The Secret of
The Kingdom of Heaven

The Secret of
The Kingdom of Heaven

DAVID CARNEGIE

Stella
Publishing

Though seeing, they do not see; though hearing, they do not hear or understand.

First published in the United Kingdom in 2007 by
Stella Publishing
176 Newbridge Road
Bath
BA1 3LE

The moral right of the author has been asserted.

ISBN 978-0-9556641-0-6

Book production by
Action Publishing Technology Limited
Gloucester GL1 5SR
Printed in Great Britain

Contents

Preface

The flight of the sparrow

In 625 A.D. King Edwin of Northumbria asked his council what they thought of this Christianity that was spreading through Europe. Paganism was strong amongst his 'witan' or council. The chief priest Coifi, a pagan, expressed the view that if the doctrine had any merit it should be adopted. Afterwards an unnamed 'thegn', or warlord, rose and said the following:

'The present life of man, O king, seems to me, in comparison of that time which is unknown to us, like to the swift flight of a sparrow through the room wherein you sit at supper in winter, with your commanders and ministers, and a good fire in the midst, whilst the storms of rain and snow prevail abroad; the sparrow, I say, flying in one door, and immediately out of another, whilst he is within, is safe from the wintry storm, but after a short space of fair weather, he immediately vanishes out of your sight, into the dark winter from which he had emerged. So this life of man appears for a short space, but of what went before; or what is to follow, we are utterly ignorant. If, therefore, this doctrine contains something more certain, it seems justly to deserve to be followed'.

Other thegns rose to express a similar sentiment and the Christian missionary Paulinus was invited to explain the doctrine to all present. So the King, his council and importantly the chief priest Coifi adopted Christianity simply because it seemed 'a good thing'. The doctrine or Truth offered a certainty or knowledge of a God that accompanied this sparrow, both in the spirit and flesh, upon its entire flight, not abandoning it either as it entered the room or at the door as it left the room. This certainty or knowledge, experienced by the mind, heart and body, allowed a man the opportunity of a life lived in the context of an eternal life; and so less fearfully and more freely. This was deemed a 'good thing'.

King Edwin's witan sought the Truth – the certainty or evidence of the presence of God's self in Man; and so the eternity of his life. Paulinus, as a Christian, offered them God's self as a trinity of persons – the Father, Son and Holy Spirit. Through his deliverance of the story of Jesus, Paulinus demonstrated the presence of this trinity of self in Man. He therefore offered evidence of a universal presence of God's self in creation, and so also in Man – a certainty in which people might then have belief, faith and trust. Paulinus delivered this Truth in an imagery and language that people of that age recognised and understood.

Jesus understood the importance of illuminating the Truth in the medium familiar to that culture and age. Events can only be explained in the context of people's existing cultural and scientific knowledge. We cannot offer explanations in terms of cultural and scientific concepts and language of which people have no knowledge. Jesus told his followers that the Truth was 'too much for them to bear and the Holy Spirit would lead them into all the Truth'. He warned his followers that the Truth was something that Man has to 'grow' into by cultural development and education.

Jesus asks his followers to 'bring forth from the storeroom old and new truths'. He is saying our doctrines and explanations have to be delivered in the imagery and language to suit the culture and age. These expressions (old and new truths) are neither wrong or right but relevant or irrelevant. They illuminate or do not illuminate. Indeed old truths (outdated imagery and language) may not only fail to illuminate but may actually hinder us from finding and growing in the Truth.

In this book the reader is invited to 'bring forth new truths', discover new relevant imagery and language for this age and so illuminate and enjoy the Truth.

Chapter One

The Trinity of Self

Jesus declared, "I am the **Way**, the **Truth** and the **Life** ... Nobody comes to (God) the Father except by me ... When you see me you see (God) the Father". Jesus claimed, as did his followers, to have God within him – and in this sense to be God. He embodied God's self, both spiritually and therefore physically in his mind (the **Truth**), his heart (the **Life**) and his body (the **Way**).

Jesus was declaring that the sense of self, as experienced by Man, is the same sense of self as God's self. The experience of self is a universal phenomenon. Everything in creation has a self or existence – from atoms to complex creatures. However everything possesses varying degrees of awareness of this universal or common sense of self. Man has the full gift of awareness or is fully aware of this sense of self – in mind, heart and body. Man therefore is described as 'being in God's image'.

Jesus' Truth (philosophy) lay in the interpretation of the nature of self. Jesus was saying that the sense of self was what gave meaning, life and so a sense of existence or fellowship to everything. Nothing, including God therefore, can exist without a sense of its own self. So Jesus gave this sense of self a sacred value, for without it all matter can have no sense of its own existence and therefore no Life. Spirit is the 'idea' or concept of something and the 'flesh' or physical is the manifestation of it. The two cannot exist apart. They are indivisible – two sides of the same coin. All creation has a common self, which is both physical and spiritual. When a tree grows, it evolves out of the common spiritual and physical self or whole. When it dies and decays it returns spiritually and physically to this self or whole. It is never conscious (as Man is) of being separate to the common self – spiritually or physically. It does, in the words of Jesus, 'the will of God' – the common self. All entities of creation, with their varying degrees of consciousness, are both a part of (share in) and possess the common self of God – and so are in 'grace' with it.

Jesus describes this union of spirit and flesh by saying, "What use is salt if it has lost its saltiness?" He says such salt is thrown away. The physical is the matter of salt and the spirit is its saltiness. If salt does not taste salty it may as well not exist as salt – and indeed cannot be called salt. Salt therefore exists as both its form and its character of saltiness. They are the same and inseparable.

In the same vein, spirit is not found without its flesh. Jesus says, "What good is a lamp or light (spirit) if it is kept under a table (out of sight), where the light it emits cannot be seen?" If we cannot see the light from the lamp, then the lamp does not exist to us. If something physical does not convey its meaning or spirit, then it is useless.

Jesus' whole Truth or philosophy hangs on this concept. Flesh is spirit and spirit is flesh. He demonstrates it with his own spirit and flesh and it lies behind his declaration, "I am the **Way**, the **Truth** and the **Life**".

Jesus describes the presence of the universal self and so unity of creation with the phrase, "Every sparrow that falls is counted". Everything in creation matters because it shares the self of God, the whole. Ninety nine per cent of baby turtles do not make it to the sea, but every single one is counted and matters to the whole. Everything is cherished. The self of God endures, lives and exists wholly through and within God's physical manifestation – every minute part of it. The creation is **holographic** in that each tiny part manifests the whole and so each part is as 'precious' or vital as the whole – only as long as it remains a part of the whole.

This holographic nature or 'preciousness' of each part is expressed in the **parable of the Good Shepherd**. The good shepherd has lost one of his sheep. He leaves all his sheep in the open and seeks the lost one until he has found it and returned it to the flock. To the shepherd each sheep is as precious as the whole flock. Each part of creation, as well as being a piece of the whole jigsaw of creation, also represents the whole jigsaw of creation – as long as it remains a part of the whole. Hence Jesus' claim of being both a man and God.

The preciousness of the sense of self (God's self) within Man is described in other stories. Jesus refers to it as a **pearl** found by a merchant who then discards all his other pearls to own this one pearl. Another story tells us of a man who finds a **treasure** (God's self within himself) in a field and sells all he has to buy this field. These stories remind us of the importance of finding this sense of self, person or spirit, which is shared by all creation, without which there is no real sense of meaning or existence. Its total value to us is expressed by the way in which the people in the story discard all other things of value in their life to possess this one thing. The Old Testament refers to the fact that Man lost his grace with God, this common self. Adam or primeval Man were like the rest of creation, in grace with the common self or, as Jesus calls it, the **Kingdom of God**. They did 'the will of God' or 'walked with God'. They were innocent, unaware or unconscious of being separate from the common self. Their sense of self was, to themselves, indistinguishable from the common sense of self. They had no concept of having a sense of self that was independent or separate from the common self or Kingdom of God. Man's birth and death was experienced as a continuum of evolving from and returning to the common self.

Human beings however possessed a 'critical mass' of consciousness or awareness of the common self. It was a full 'inheritance' or potentially a complete awareness of the common self. In this way they were 'in the image of God' or Sons of God – intellectually, emotionally and physically.

The fall from grace or **Original Sin** was the moment when an individual (Adam and Eve) became fully conscious of the common self within them. They became self conscious. This full consciousness is the proverbial 'tree of knowledge of good and evil'. With this complete consciousness of the common self comes the immediate temptation to 'eat of the tree of knowledge', to take personal possession of the common self or 'inheritance', to take independence and view this sense of self as your own. It is the moment of loss of innocence or this 'unawareness' of the inheritance within. It is when Man realises the true magnitude of what this sense of self can convey – a sense of personal identity, life and meaning of one's own. Man sets up shop on his own and prodigal Man is born.

In the story of Genesis the first human beings, Adam and Eve, commit this sin. Eve is credited with being the one approached by the Temptation. It is because this knowledge, consciousness or self awareness of what Man had within, would have appeared to convey great advantage to the human race – a command of the common self or to be God like. A female human may well have been the first to take this full awareness of the common self for herself (and so fall from grace with it) due to her own enhanced desire to attain any advantage for her offspring.

Jesus tells the **parable of the Prodigal Son** to show how Man takes his inheritance (his own sense of self) and leaves the Kingdom (common sense of self). Man, on becoming aware of what he possesses or has inherited, wants to personally possess it. Man now identifies himself as separate by giving each person a name. Man becomes aware of birth and death, each event now being accompanied by emotional, intellectual and physical pain. All mothers give birth with a joy tinged with sadness (the baby blues). Death is experienced as a profound loss. Man is no longer innocently in grace and must rely purely on his own sense of self (rather than share in the common self) – on his own instinct, intuition and effort. Prodigal Man or Fallen Man perceived, felt and experienced a sense of abandonment, a sense of being on his own – apart from the common self. Man is 'cast from the Kingdom'. Innocence as 'unawareness' cannot be regained or reinstated. Our knowledge or awareness becomes a natural and inherited condition, passed from parent to child. Prodigal self builds a prodigal world to suit. The temptation to maintain an 'ownership' of a sense of self is overwhelming, once Man is conscious or has knowledge that he can.

Man is aware of having made a mistake or committing a sin. He becomes aware of a lack of grace and a feeling of separation. He tries to bridge the gap between himself and the common sense of self with religion. This takes the form of sacrifice (bribing God), worship (appeasing God) and rules (pleasing God). None of these help Man or give Man peace or grace with the common self. For three hundred years before Jesus people prophesied that a man would come who would bring 'not more laws but grace' – a Messiah. This Messiah would bring 'salvation' – a way in which prodigal self could find grace with God or the universal self. He would set the prodigal 'free', from being a victim of its isolation. He would bring help for the prodigal.

Jesus expresses his own grace with the words – "I am given all by the Father, for I have given all to the Father". The prodigal self of Man can have grace with the self of God, the universal self. He can have the help of the Father and 'all that the Father has'. He can have a sharing in the universal self of God (The Kingdom) **and** have his prodigal self or awareness. With this help from the Father, this sharing, Man can do the 'will of God'. Jesus describes his grace as, "I only do what I see the Father doing". Man can lose his innocence and 'still walk with God' – still share in the Kingdom or common self. Man can be **redeemed** from being on his own.

Jesus explains his **Truth** or philosophy in a language that people could understand or comprehend. However he struggled to convey the Truth because he had to convey not something that could be comprehended by their prodigal selves but something new about the very nature of self. It is hard for people to comprehend or perceive something which they can only comprehend if they radically change their own notion of self, of who and what they are. Jesus tells his followers to be careful – "Do not cast your pearls before swine, because they will trample them underfoot". This Truth is not something that can be forced onto people who are not willing or prepared to receive it. It is not a 'classroom' Truth or philosophy. People have to be 'born again', or have to change their view of 'self' itself, in order to receive this 'pearl'. In another story Jesus spent a whole night trying to explain the Truth to Nicodemus, a highly intelligent lawyer. Jesus used the expression, 'The Kingdom of Heaven', to explain the universal sense of self – God's self. He explained that salvation lay within us – in our sense of self. God's self was within us. He proclaimed that "The Kingdom of Heaven is within us ... The Kingdom of Heaven is among us ... The Kingdom of Heaven is coming ..." God's mind, heart and fellowship/body are within us as individuals and universal amongst all creation and Jesus was here to reveal it.

Jesus prepared people to radically change their notion of self, with the profound riddle, "He who tries to save his life (self) will lose his life (self) and he who gives up his life (self) for my sake (the Holy Spirit) will gain his life (the Kingdom of Heaven or common self of God). Jesus here is defining the common self in holographic terms. If we are prepared to become a part of the Kingdom or common self and share in it, we gain all of it, whilst still remaining a part. If we want to remain separate to it we lose it. Jesus talks of the Kingdom also as a vine. If we remain a part or branch of the vine we will have life but if the branch becomes separate from the vine it withers.

John, the gospel writer, explains the Truth or the true nature of self in his words – "The Truth shall set you free". Jesus says himself, "I have come to set you free". We are searching for the Truth or the existence of God's self as something (whether in a perfect God/religion or perfect man/Jesus) outside and separate to ourselves – only to discover that it is within us, in our very own sense of self. We are released from a prison of being a prodigal Son, fruitlessly searching for God the Father 'out there' to help us. Instead we find the Father, the Son and the Spirit of their Love (Holy Spirit) within our own self. How can this be? Jesus reveals that the sense of self, as all things, has a both spiritual and physical nature – a Trinity. God's self, as all self, is a trinity of persons. Jesus reveals the nature of self with a famous story – the **story of the Prodigal Son**. In this story Jesus describes a Kingdom in which a Father and Son live together. They share or co-own the Kingdom. The Son asks for his share or 'inheritance' of the Kingdom so he can leave and go his own way. The Father gives him what is rightfully his half of the Kingdom. The Father and Son both own and occupy the whole Kingdom (and enjoy a whole sense of self or ownership of the Kingdom) but if one person wants to leave, this Kingdom or whole sense of self, has to be split between the two of them – being also physical in nature. So the prodigal Son leaves with his half share. The word 'prodigal' means wasteful. He is wasteful because he has wasted or lost ownership of the whole Kingdom and ended up with half of it – which he soon finds out is useless to him.

The prodigal Son finds that his inheritance does not sustain him and he ends up alone and destitute in a pigsty, looking after pigs. He remembers his Father's kingdom and decides to return to it. The Father sees his return and comes out to show his delight. The Son expects to be given a very menial job in the Kingdom befitting his bankrupt status, similar to the pigsty work. The Father embraces this bankrupt Son and sets out a party to celebrate his homecoming. He kills his prize fatted calf, which in Jesus' culture, would have been a symbol of the highest honour bestowed upon a guest. It was a most treasured possession and a symbol of complete sharing with the guest.

The dutiful Son, who never left the Kingdom, is angry that his prodigal brother seems to be rewarded for his sin of betrayal. He refuses to join the celebration. However the Father goes out to see him and reassures this son that he is always with the Father, and that everything the Father has is already his. He celebrates the return of his prodigal Son because 'once he was lost and now he is found'. The prodigal Son has returned purely 'of his own accord' – by his own will and so his own love. The Father has reciprocated this with His own will and love. The story is Jesus' explanation of the peculiar nature of self – as a trinity of persons – the persons of the Father, Son and Holy Spirit (or person of free will or love freely given). Both the persons of the Father and Son share the Kingdom (a single sense of self); something only made possible (spiritually and therefore physically) by their common free will or commitment to do so in the separate person of the Holy Spirit. The Father and Son both have a 'free will' or share a common Spirit or person of free will to either share the Kingdom or leave the Kingdom – to leave or return. This shared Spirit is therefore the Holy Spirit or Spirit of Love voluntarily or freely given – rather than conditional love that seeks a reward or fears consequences or retribution. It is the person or Spirit that unites the two persons of the Father and Son and makes them one person, Spirit, self or Kingdom. The Father and Son are not made one by their separate and identical natures/persona but by their separate and free, but identical wills. However because this Spirit is one of free will, it allows the separation of itself into the identical wills of the Father and Son, if that is the will of either. However the Father and Son cannot be separated from their own wills and so their share in the Spirit of free love – the Holy Spirit. **See Figure 1 – The United Kingdom of God's Self and Figure 2 – The Divided Kingdom of Prodigal Self.**

The nature of God's self as three persons is not a mystery but has a philosophical logic or **Truth.** Any being, even God as an all powerful and infinite being, has to have a sense of self. If it does not have a sense of self then it cannot have a sense of being, existence or as Jesus describes it – **Life.** In order to have a sense of self a being must have a 'reflection' of what it is. This reflection of itself must be a being separate and independent to itself and yet capable of reflecting **all** that it is (i.e. identical to it). So the concept of the Father and Son is born, the two separate but identical beings/persons. The Father gives all that He

FIGURE I
The United Kingdom of God's Self

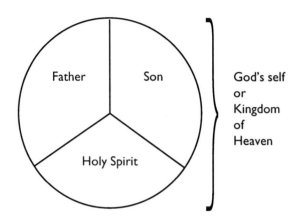

God's self
or
Kingdom
of
Heaven

FIGURE 2
The Divided Kingdom of Prodigal Self

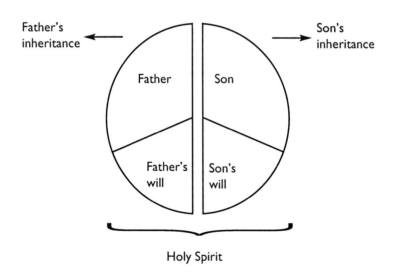

has (a perfect reflection or glorification as Jesus calls it) to the Son and vice versa. Both therefore acquire a perfect or accurate sense of who they are (a sense of self) or who they share – by virtue of each other's reflection. The Father and Son must be completely separate beings to each other otherwise they cannot act as a true 'reflection' of what each other is. Who then is the Holy Spirit? Again there is logic to the person or Spirit of free will. In order for God to have a sense of self, God's self must have a will to acquire such a thing – a desire to be. Because the Father and Son must be separate persons they have to retain their own separate wills. Two beings may be identical but that does not make them one being. They become one being or person by their separate and so free wills, being joined in one will. So the Will is a separate entity or person that the Father and Son share in – a person which unifies them and in which they are unified.

So the Father and Son both own a 'share' in the person of free will, from which they cannot be separated. It is part of each being's person or inheritance. Their separate wills can be used to perfectly reflect or freely love each other and so be one, or reject each other and become separate persons.

When the Father and Son freely love and give all to each other in the Spirit or person of free will (the Holy Spirit) there arises a common sense of self – God's self or Kingdom of Heaven. When the Son (in theory either the Father or Son) rejects the Father, this prodigal Son must seek a 'new' Father, join their wills and so glorify or reflect themselves in order to have a common sense of self. This Father will be a 'prodigal' Father of the prodigal Son's own making and desire.

So Jesus defined God's self, as the three persons or Spirits of the Father, Son and Holy Spirit, joined in one. Self cannot exist in any other form (except as a prodigal delusion) and Jesus defined Man's true experience of self in the same terms. The sense of self can only arise out of a free will, desire or love given and received. Without this Holy Spirit there is no existence or Life – even for God.

The prodigal Son, on leaving the Kingdom, splits the will of the Holy Spirit and leaves the Father's will behind. In order to have a kingdom or sense of self, the prodigal Son has to fill the place of the Father and His Will with an image of a father and his (father's) will of his own choosing and fabrication. He has to join wills with this father and both glorify (reflect) and be glorified by his father. This 'person' of the father is chosen at birth and is the person who the prodigal Child sees as the person 'in charge', or who gives that child life. It is the physical or earthly father, mother, guardian or sibling. In the story of the prodigal Son, the prodigal Son is badly let down by what he places in his Father's half. His prodigal father lets him down and he becomes alone, abandoned and destitute. He decides to seek out his Father's Kingdom again.

The returning prodigal Son has lost all his confidence and does not expect any standing in the Kingdom. He has after all ruined and wasted what the Father had given him. He has betrayed his Father's love completely with an irreversible loss of innocence both spiritually and physically. He does not expect to be of much use to his Father. However he finds that his Father is a person of supreme kindness – full of infinite patience and understanding. He is a Father who cannot do anything but love and forgive all those that ask – a person pure and without guile. The Father cannot restore the prodigal Son back to innocence but can offer him all that He has in terms of His love, support and help. He lays Himself at His Son's disposal, prodigal and bankrupt or not.

The Son has returned to put things right with his Father in whatever way he can. He will do the lowliest of jobs if necessary. He has little and expects little. He approaches his Father's Kingdom with absolute humility, knowing that he cannot offer anything as he is bankrupt and has squandered everything. He cannot reflect or glorify the Father as he did before when he was a dutiful and innocent son.

Yet the Father welcomes this crippled Son into the grace of His Kingdom by virtue of their love alone. Here we see the power of the Holy Spirit or person of Love – its ability to restore. Jesus refers to this person as the **Helper**. It restores by offering help. It has a total and absolute power to create grace between the Father and Son. Jesus describes this power with the words, "All things are possible with God". The prodigal Son presents himself to the Father in the person of the Holy Spirit, with absolute humility, asking for help and forgiveness. The Father responds in the person of the Holy Spirit by giving what is required to help His bankrupt Son, from His own infinite wealth.

We see the nature of the Holy Spirit here as the Helper. He is privy to the Father's and the Son's natures, intentions and needs, being a composite of their wills. He knows what each has, what each needs and how best the common interest of both can be met – how best to help. He does not make suggestions or execute grace without the full permission of the Father and Son's wills. Jesus always talks of the need for humility on the part of the prodigal Son, because he has to be aware of his own need for the Holy Spirit to respond. Humility is knowledge of the reality of bankruptcy. The prodigal Son has to give his own permission to be helped by the Helper. The prodigal Son gives this permission by his own humility. The more humble he is the more help is given. The Helper will not respond to what the prodigal Son wants but what he needs – so that He (the Helper) can reflect or glorify the Father. In the story the prodigal Son's humility (love) is rewarded by the Holy spirit with a fatted calf from the Father's wealth (His love). Any help the prodigal Son receives he attributes to the Father – he glorifies the Father with it. We see Jesus doing just this, when he says, "I only do what I see the Father doing". He attributes all that he does to be gifts from the Father by virtue of the Holy Spirit. So in spite of all the irreversible Sin that the prodigal Son has committed he can be healed and restored from the wealth of the Father by their shared love in the person of the Holy Spirit alone – the Father's generosity and the prodigal Son's humility.

The dutiful Son, who remained with the Father in the

Kingdom and whose will remains with the Father's will, is suddenly and unexpectedly angry. He turns his back on the Father and withdraws his will from the Holy Spirit. He refuses his prodigal brother. The dutiful and faithful Son has remained innocent and unaware of his inheritance and own free will. He has never been tempted to do anything but innocently reciprocate the Father's will. By forgiving the prodigal Son the person of the Holy Spirit and Father reveal their natures to the faithful Son and in particular the blessing of free will – the total freedom to love and not love. The dutiful Son is enlightened of his own self by the Father's treatment of the returning prodigal Son. He becomes aware or conscious of his own person and will as separate to that of the Father. We see the Father and dutiful Son now have to renew their commitment consciously with each other – their unity of wills in the person of the Holy Spirit. The Father says to the dutiful Son that he appreciates his unity and loyalty and he always has His loyalty – "All that I have is yours and always will be". They both accept the return of the prodigal Son into the Kingdom, his humility, his request for forgiveness and grace and his unity in the Holy Spirit with the Father.

Here we see the prodigal Son expecting to 'pay' for his return to the Kingdom. The Father however restores the Kingdom to him as a free gift. Both the prodigal and faithful Son learn that the Kingdom is not a reward but something freely entered into – by love, for love and nothing else.

The humility of the prodigal Son is reciprocated by the unconditional kindness of the Father, in the unity of the Helper. The theme of restoration and grace by humility and kindness alone is repeated again and again in the teaching of Jesus. In the **parable of the Sower** the good soil is the only 'person' who is humble in all his soul, in his mind, heart and body – and so receives the kindness of the Father in mind, heart and body by the grace (help) of the Holy Spirit. On the cross the robber beside Jesus shows absolute humility as a prodigal Son and in doing so receives kindness of the Father by the grace or help of the Holy Spirit. Even in his last moments he is saved by his own humility alone, being in no position to repair any of the damage he has done. Salvation is granted to him then and there as Jesus says, "Today you shall be with me in paradise (the Kingdom)". Jesus tells the Pharisees (the great and the good) that sinners and prostitutes (the reviled) were getting into the Kingdom before them. This is because it is not righteousness, sacrifice or penance but humility that saves us.

Jesus reminds his followers that in their humility (knowledge of their prodigal nature) they have to ask for unity in the Holy Spirit – with the Father's kindness. Humility must be their will. "Seek and ye shall find. Knock and the door shall be opened". The Father's will responds only to the prodigal Sons' humility – not to someone's feeling they have got to return, or want to, or ought to, or because they fear the consequences if they do not. The prodigal 'freely' returns by his own will alone and not the Father's.

In the **parable of the vineyard** it is not what the workers did that each got paid for. They were paid for turning up for work alone and each received the same pay – the absolute kindness of the Father in the unity of the Holy Spirit. The worker, as the prodigal Son, is paid for 'turning up for work' – which is an offering of his humility. The Father offers 'all that He has' and withholds nothing. All receive the same pay.

The extent of the Father's Love is described by Jesus in the Sermon on the Mount. – "Love your enemy. Do good to those that harm you. Lend without any thought of return. If someone steals your coat, give him your shirt too. Give to anyone anything they ask ..." This is not a naive call to a fanciful utopia or impossible dream; nor is it a call to social, economic and political suicide or anarchy. Jesus is showing every human, whatever their piety, righteousness or achievement that they are prodigal and in need of absolute humility in their unity with such a loving Father. Nothing the prodigal Son can do in terms of his own works can come anywhere near reflecting or glorifying the Father. It also reassures people of the Father's absolute generosity, forgiveness and help – what they can expect in return for their absolute humility in the unity or grace of the Holy Spirit.

The prodigal Son can only glorify what the Father is by virtue of his own absolute humility.

The comprehension or Truth that the sense of self is a Trinity of persons (Father, Son and Holy Spirit of free will) is what separates Christianity from all other religions and philosophies. It sets it apart as something 'other worldly'. Jesus said to Pilate who failed to recognise it, "My Kingdom is of another world". No other religion or philosophy describes the concept of self as something that is both spiritual and physical and which emerges from the mutual glorification of Father and Son by a common but separate Spirit of free will. No other religion entertains the reality of granting healing and restoration to the prodigal self by the Holy Spirit – the opportunity for redemption by the act of mutual love alone, not mercy. Redemption, or grace, comes by this mutual and free sharing of humility and kindness between Father and Son by virtue of the person of the Holy Spirit, the Spirit of Love.

Jesus says to his followers, "Nobody comes to the Father except by me". He is alluding to the presence of the Father, Son and Holy Spirit within himself. He is the prodigal Son who serves faithfully his humility, and so is served with all that the Father has through the Holy Spirit; he therefore has the unity of the Father, Son and Holy Spirit within him – God's self. Yet when Jesus is called 'good' he rejects this label with the words, "Do not call me good for only God is good". Jesus is rejecting, as the prodigal Son, any idea that any righteousness comes from him. It all comes from a consequence of knowledge of his own bankruptcy – that he is not good. All that he has comes from the Father through the help of the Holy Spirit. So Jesus does call on people to be 'perfect as the Father is perfect', but here he means perfectly humble and forgiving. He goes on to say that people should 'cut out an eye if it offends them for it is better to enter the Kingdom eyeless than not enter at all'. By this he means 'purge yourself of anything that comes between you and your absolute humility for this, not purity, is what will gain you the help of the Holy Spirit'.

When some people, who accepted the power and reality of the prodigal Son's humility in the Holy Spirit, came to Jesus, they asked him, "What should we do now?" Jesus replied, "Go give freely as you have been given freely". Jesus was saying to them that their humility had saved them and earned them the kindness of the Father and help (grace) of the Holy Spirit. Go and share that experience of grace with others – its humility of the prodigal Son, kindness of the Father and help of the Holy Spirit.

Jesus describes this help or grace as 'an eternal spring that flows from within and never dries up'. "We shall thirst no more". But the arrogant prodigal Son with a prodigal father thirsts endlessly for acknowledgement, love and caring. He is persistently let down, disillusioned, disappointed and in the end abandoned.

Jesus also refers to this grace as the vine (Kingdom) and the prodigal Son as a branch of the vine. If the prodigal Son remains humble, he remains a part of the vine and will be fed by the trunk of the vine (the Father's kindness). If the prodigal Son, as a branch, becomes separated from the vine, then he will wither without the trunk.

Jesus was introducing a philosophy or Truth that was blasphemous. People could not testify on behalf of God, claim to be God or in grace with God. Such philosophy is treated with ridicule today but in Jesus' time it was punishable by death. People believed in a God's self that was singular and lay outside Man. Man gained entrance to the Kingdom of God by following a code of righteousness and through the mercy obtained by sacrifice and penance. People lived in theocracies, where a ticket to the Kingdom could be won by following a lifestyle or instruction manual. People could be 'chosen' by even just believing in the book. Jesus declared that no–one could enter the Kingdom or be 'chosen' by following a righteousness laid down in a book or religion. People had to be 'born again' in the Spirit and realise God's kingdom (God's self) within them. This could only occur by the opposite to religious righteousness – absolute humility. Jesus declared that he had not come to bring 'peace (unity) but a sword'. He was not coming to serve a religion but the Truth – grace.

Chapter Two

Satan and the Three Forms of Prodigal Son

Jesus describes all the sickness of Man (in mind, heart and body) as coming from the prodigal self or divided self. The Spirit or person of the departing prodigal Son goes it alone and this is none other than the Spirit or person of Satan and his Temptations.

The Spirit or person of Satan takes three forms, each form describing the half self of the Kingdom or self of God, the prodigal Son and his share of the person of free will or Holy Spirit. The Father and his share of the person of will are left behind with the dutiful Son.

So within people we can see three different forms of Satan who is the arrogant prodigal self or half self. The prodigal Son half is pronounced and evident and the Father's half is ignored, rejected or absent (both spiritually and physically). For the prodigal Son now sees the Father as something outside himself and of his own fabrication.

These three forms are the **Brute** (the mythological Minotaur), **Lucifer** and the **Snake**. These are the physical likenesses of these 'half' or prodigal selves. They are best described diagrammatically. The self of mind, heart and body is literally divided in two – both spiritually and physically. **See Figure 3 – describing Lucifer, Figure 4 – describing The Snake** and **Figure 5 describing The Brute.**

Lucifer describes the satanic form which has prodigal ownership of the heart and a half a mind, but lacks ownership of the body and half mind, which lies with the Father. It is also repre-

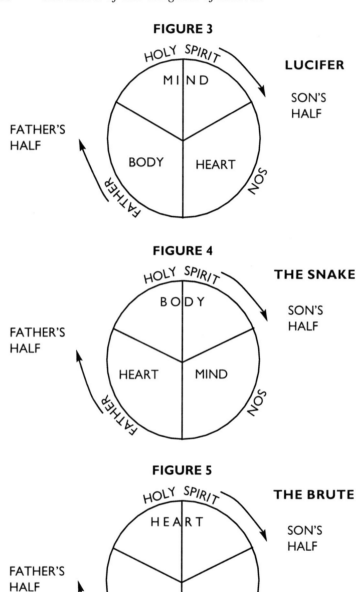

FIGURE 3

FIGURE 4

FIGURE 5

sented in mythology by the **sirens**, which are physically elusive, bodiless creatures who lure sailors to their deaths with a promise of love (pleasure and song).

These are the prodigal personalities who are charming, warm hearted, affectionate and seductive. They make romantic (physically generous) lovers, who are playful and fun loving, often practical jokers. They are emotionally sentimental and wear their 'hearts on their sleeves'. They are the hearty, 'hail well met' types. They often have a passion or love for speed, fast cars, engine power or a fascination for flying, which are all expressive of the physicality or expansiveness of their prodigal heart. They can also be the pessimistic 'doomsters and killjoys' who always fear something going wrong with the heart.

In their 'absent' Father half they will live out the fellowship/body vicariously through others outside themselves. They lure and beckon others into their fellowship or body and half mind (Father's half). They do this in order literally to have a spiritual and physical body! They are therefore very clubbable people. They 'beg, borrow and steal' from others' bodies and fellowships. They will often ask for and borrow money. They will often fill their homes with physical clutter and half completed activities and projects.

These people can be 'absent minded', elusive, unreliable and uncommunicative in the fellowship/body (their Father). They are 'accident prone' or conversely incautious and risk takers and gamblers with material things, other people and their own bodies. They are therefore prone to make misjudgements and inappropriate actions for which they are very heartfelt apologetic afterwards. This is exactly how Peter the apostle (a prodigal heart) lets down Jesus by three times denying him, or denying being a follower of him. Peter wept.

They are divided in the mind (their Holy Spirit) and so will use opinions and ideas simply to justify the passions of their prodigal heart, rather than any general accepted logic. They are therefore often garrulous, erratic, argumentative, disorganised and prone to flights of fancy.

When they suffer moments of stress or insecurity they will defend themselves by attacking with their prodigal heart. They heap ridicule and mockery on their opponents which are both forms of emotional belittlement and torture. Otherwise they will withdraw, become emotional and cry and storm off. If they suffer prolonged stress to the point of developing a neurotic condition, this will take the form of the repetitive behaviour of a frightened prodigal heart trying desperately to find emotional reassurance of itself by bewailing the absence of the Father. They become the habitual 'doomsters' that emotionally bemoan constantly the state of the world (really the absence of fellowship/body within themselves), which they put down to a lack of principles or the love of the prodigal heart. If stress goes beyond neurosis, bipolar depression can develop where the Father and Son become dislocated from one another and they become 'split personalities'. The stress on the prodigal becomes too much to bear and it is 'shared' between the Father and Son. These people will express this illness as a violent mood swing from 'ecstatic delusions of grandeur', representing the Father's greatness of body, and emotional self reproach and disgust, representing an abandoned, isolated and crippled prodigal heart. If they suffer stress to the point of insanity, this split personality will become exaggerated to a socially unacceptable level. They will actually become alternately their own figures of grandeur and empire, such as Napoleon, and then opposing figures of emotional self disgust who they emotionally abuse with threats and foul language. If they suffer exhaustion it will express itself as emotional exhaustion. They become tired and emotional.

When such people find the Father within them, they become the 'rocks' of the church or faith. They are natural fellowship builders and often literally become church builders. They make good priests by virtue of their protection and understanding of the body/fellowship of God's self – a fellowship where everyone and everything is equally precious. They attract people with their warmth of heart. They can be, in the absence of the Holy Spirit (being born again) the zealous 'lion hearts' or crusaders in their quest historically to physically construct the fellowship, defending that fellowship to the death, but using themselves and everyone else as cannon fodder (a lack of fellowship/body) in the process.

Peter belonged to this prodigal type and was the crusading hot head who cut off the soldier's ear in his defence of Jesus when he was arrested. Peter was chosen by Jesus to 'feed his sheep' and was the 'rock' upon which he wanted his church or fellowship to be built. Peter in his martyrdom was crucified upside down, symbolic of a piece of meat or body of an animal in a butcher's shop. He symbolised the body of God.

The **Snake** describes the satanic form which has prodigal ownership of the mind and half body. In mythological terms it is the **serpent in the Garden of Eden** putting forward the false idea or fiction that, 'eating of the tree of knowledge' or throwing off innocence, will bring the personal power of God to Adam and Eve. Instead it brings a fall from grace for the prodigal Son. These are the personalities who are the thinkers and schemers who have a heightened sense of their own logic. They apply self made theories to life and so see life through the logic of their mind. These people will attach themselves to all sorts of theories, ideas or 'truths' spawned by the power of the prodigal mind. They are proponents and victims of all sorts of wacky unproven alternative remedies, diets and spiritualities, ranging from crystal ball gazing to tarot card reading.

In the 'absent' Father' half they will live vicariously through others – beg, borrow and steal other's emotions (as Lucifer does the fellowship). They are often seen as the 'bleeding hearts' of society, fighting against a perceived injustice and for an imagined world of peace and love. They portray therefore an air of saintliness or righteousness. They are however prone to be unreliable, uncommunicative, inconsistent or elusive in their emotional lives. They are often the figureheads of spiritual cults and sects, religions and ideologies as Hitler was for Nazism. They have the ability to inspire (steal) the love, worship and devotion of others for the construction of a moral or mental superiority. They are able to do this by weaving, using 'smoke and mirrors' (the power of the prodigal mind), a deceptive picture of themselves or any notion, and so trick people into following them or that notion. They are therefore inspirational leaders who get caught up in their own tricks. They are also prone to be followers themselves and deceive themselves. All these prodigal minds are looking for fictional people and causes to find their absent heart in – to be loved and to love, to worship and be worshipped.

Their half ownership of the fellowship/body (the Holy Spirit) may be dictated to one moment by vicarious emotion (the Father) and the next by the cold logic of the prodigal mind. They are untrustworthy in the fellowship and will always seek an opportunity to 'make easy money', exploit a weakness in the system, or spin a trick for their own advantage.

When they suffer moments of stress or insecurity they will defend the prodigal mind like a snake, seeking out with deadly accuracy the vulnerabilities of people with cruel moral judgements – sometimes a 'disdainful' look suffices. Their attack is deigned to poison, to mentally hurt and torture. They alternately become withdrawn and 'moody' and slam the door in people's faces. If they suffer prolonged stress to the point of causing a neurotic condition, this will take the form of a desire to maintain a 'perfect' righteousness (prodigal mind). They will link their survival to certain complicated, even bizarre rituals, theories, life style choices, therapies or diets, of which they claim a significance that far outweighs their actual significance. They will bemoan the lack of love and justice in the world (actually the lack of the Father in themselves). If stress precipitates a bipolar depression (or split personality of Father and Son) it takes the form of manic swings between emotionally ecstatic elation (the Father's heart) where they may go on sprees of 'emotional abandonment' and irresponsible flights of fancy (often helping themselves to people's property as if it were communal property) to severe thoughts of self reproach and disgust and suicidal thoughts (self reproach of the abandoned prodigal mind). If they suffer stress to the point of insanity then this split personality will become exaggerated to a socially unacceptable state where they will become, or lose themselves in, the Father's heart in the form of a delusion which may include thinking they are a Messiah of Love and then become persons of self disgust; this may take the form of actual self harm (cutting etc). If they suffer exhaustion it always expresses itself as mental exhaustion. This may manifest itself as such psychologically induced (but physically real) ailments as M.E.

When such people find the Father within, they become the martyrs who go to their deaths, like lambs (Jesus was called the Lamb of God), both protecting and defining the heart of the church – the love of God. Jesus himself was a prodigal mind and was symbolically crucified, baring his heart to the world and having it pierced by a spear. These people form the heart of the church – diligent, dutiful, loyal and consistent in their prayer and worship. They make the nuns and monks of the church with their quiet courage, loyalty and patience. They often make better support workers in a church rather than priests – encouraging people to prayer and worship. However they also make up the people who can, in the absence of the Holy Spirit (being born again) interpret 'pure in heart' to be a call to a prodigal righteousness and religion rather than prodigal humility and as a result can become 'crusaders' of a cruel (heartless) and over zealous righteousness (prodigal mind).

Thomas was such a prodigal type who, for all his righteousness and loyalty, let down Jesus in the end by refusing to believe in his spirit, even when it stood before him. However in the end he travelled further and more bravely than any disciple to establish Christianity in India.

The **Brute** describes the satanic form which has the prodigal ownership of the body and half heart. In mythological terms this form is the **Minotaur** (half man half beast) who crashes blindly and energetically, around lost in a maze (representative of his absent mind). These are the 'doers', cyborgs or busy bees of the prodigal world. They have a heightened sense of their own bodies and so they express themselves with great energy and are very active, noisy and talkative – often prone to making a running commentary. They like getting things done and solving physical problems with actions, rather than applying the mind.

In the absent Father they live their mental lives vicariously through others, begging, borrowing and stealing other's opinions. They are often therefore opinionated, talkative and noisy – like an empty vessel that makes much noise. They are the proverbial 'bull in a china shop'. They are mentally elusive and so, in some ways, appear unreal and unconvincing, offering many opinions but sticking to none. They are at worst the opinionated do-gooders or busy bodies of the world. They will swap horses in mid stream (betray) with seeming ease and justification.

Their half prodigal hearts are unreliable as they are dictated to by their prodigal bodies, rather than the mind. They can be therefore (unconvincingly) charming in a slick and smarmy way or severe; emotionally diffident or passionate. They blow hot and cold in the heart.

When they suffer moments of stress or insecurity they defend the frightened prodigal body by being physically aggressive and lashing out, or express their fear for the prodigal body inwardly as hypochondria (fear of losing the body). If this stress is prolonged enough to precipitate a neurotic condition, this will express itself as compulsive repetitive action which may be any tasks (often include cleaning and washing). The sufferer will literally go 'around in circles' for no reason – like the Minotaur in the maze. If the stress continues to the point where a bipolar depression or personality split occurs (between Father and Son) then it will take the form of manic swings of mood between ecstatic visions of the Truth (the unity of creation) coupled with the gifts of prophesy (the Father's mind) and almost catatonic states of inactivity and sensations of uselessness and pointlessness (self reproach of the abandoned prodigal body). If this stress precipitates insanity, the bipolar depression becomes so acute that its exaggeration creates socially unacceptable behaviour. These people will manically live out their visions of Truth and may even think they are God or some visionary, then collapse into excitable paranoia or real catatonic states of physical paralysis. If they suffer a bout of exhaustion it will take the form of 'nervous exhaustion' or a physical collapse.

When these prodigal Sons find the Father they become the visionaries and evangelists, like John the writer of Revelations or John the Baptist who 'paved the way' for Jesus. John the Baptist was symbolically decapitated, not martyring his body like Peter or his heart like Jesus, but his head. These people are the evangelists who interpret the message of the Trinity for the times and shine a light to the road ahead. They often have the gift of prophesy because of their grasp of the Truth. These people can best describe and protect the mind of God's self, the Trinity. They bear the 'sword of Truth'. They interpret the times. However, in the absence of the Holy Spirit (being born again) they can in their zealousness for action often interpret the message or story pragmatically or to suit their own perceived goals. They will therefore be willing to betray principles and appear to change sides if it appears pragmatic to do so – a characteristic Jesus used in Judas to 'fulfil his own destiny'.

Humour is a great revelation of the prodigal self. It is where people make light of the seriousness of their prodigal condition. There are therefore three distinct forms of humour.

Slapstick humour makes fun or 'light' of the absence of the body in Lucifer and is most enjoyed by the prodigal hearts. Clever **irony** makes fun of the absence of the heart in the snake and is most appreciated by the prodigal mind. **Sarcasm** (aptly called the lowest form of wit or cleverness) makes fun of the absence of the mind in the Brute and is most appreciated by the prodigal body. These forms of wit are best employed by the people who suffer the appropriate prodigal self. We watch Laurel and Hardy, prodigal hearts, do warm hearted slap stick (practical joking). Jack Dee and Sacha Baron, as prodigal minds serve us great irony. We watch Graucho Marx, Bill Connolly and Alan Partridge strut their stuff energetically delivering a most bizarre form of sarcasm.

There is one further form of comedy – **situation comedy or farce.** This comedy makes light of the absence of fellowship or social structures. In this comedy the security of having a fellowship or society falls apart or breaks down and we laugh. It laughs at the exposure, failure or absence of the collective body – the church. This form of humour is most appreciated by institutions and families that are caught up and weighed down by rigid social structure. It is appreciated by all prodigal types and is best enjoyed collectively.

The popularity of the clown lies in its theatrical mastery of and encapsulation of all the four types of comedy – slapstick, irony, sarcasm and farce. The clown therefore has something of the complete pathos and soul of Mankind within it – both our collective and individual awkwardness of the three prodigal selves. We enjoy and delight in the clown making light of us all.

All humour therefore is an important way in which we shed for a moment the 'weight' of our prodigal selves and reflects a deep instinct to find some relief from the burden.

Drama or theatre also reveals and reflects the prodigal selves – whatever the medium. Writers instinctively describe with their scripts the different prodigal selves. All scripts and stories play out the dramas of the prodigal natures of Man, where actors are cast to play a prodigal type (more often than not their own). However the copying of a character is achieved by the Father self.

Prodigal hearts are good 'situation' actors and maintain and create a strong bodily presence on stage – actors such as Richard Burton, Sylvester Stallone and John Travolta. They are great **instinctive** actors who use the knowledge of the body to make a convincing copy of their character. Prodigal bodies like Marlon Brando, Tom Cruise or James Roberston Justice have a great mental presence on stage. They are the **'method'** actors who use belief, or present a mental picture, to create a convincing copy of the character. Prodigal minds like Clint Eastwood and Tom Hanks have a great emotional presence on stage. They are the great **intuitive** actors who use the knowledge of the heart to create a convincing picture of the character. They all draw on the knowledge of the Father self to project a convincing prodigal self. In this way the prodigal selves are 'thrown' or projected as whole, real and three dimensional.

Even cartoons portray the prodigal selves, albeit two dimensional. In the **Simpsons** we see the warm hearted but accident prone Homer, a prodigal heart, alongside Marge as the efficient busy prodigal body. Lisa is well portrayed as a prodigal mind with her 'bleeding heart', her prodigal self suggesting Homer is made the 'key parent' or prodigal father. Bart follows in his father's footsteps as the fun loving prodigal heart, his prodigal heart taking up centre stage in the family, as it often does. Maggie follows as a young, but recognisable, prodigal body like her mother (always wanting to copy her busy mother).

A casual glance at the script for the film, **Braveheart**, reveals a great unfolding drama of the prodigal selves. We see the prodigal heart of Wallace (Mel Gibson) juxtaposed against the prodigal mind of Robert Bruce (Angus McFadyen). Both are drawn into a fight for Scotland, but we see two different approaches – Wallace's passion (for personal revenge too) and recklessness against Bruce's careful weighing of the situation. Wallace is impetuous and a risk taker, speaking from the heart while Bruce carefully studies the whole picture and treads cautiously. In the end Wallace appeals to Bruce's 'heart' and Bruce takes up the baton in the form of a 'noble and just cause' for Scotland – and wins. We see in the film a number of key nobles who are prodigal bodies who switch sides when it is prudent and profitable to do so.

If the script is studied, each prodigal type betrays itself by its own language. On the issue of the rebellion we hear Wallace say to Bruce, "Its all for nothing if you do not have freedom". Freedom is a physical thing for Wallace and he always describes the way to get it is to 'fight' for it, using the word over and over again like a crusader. He cares little for his physical body when he answers Bruce's caution with, "All men die: the question is how and why". Again he says, "Everyman dies, not every man really lives". Bruce on the other hand is suspicious of passion (the prodigal heart in Wallace). He takes Wallace aside and says, "Now I know you've sacrificed much. But fighting these odds looks like rage, not courage". Wallace replies by appealing to Bruce's Father in the heart, something beyond and deeper than prodigal passion. He says, "It is well **beyond** rage. Help me. For Christ's sake help yourselves. If we join we win. If we win; well then we'll have what none of us has ever had before; a country of our own". Wallace has gone beyond passion to a conviction, a vision, an idea or spirit of Scotland. His 'fight' now is about the right of any human being for respect and value. This is what Bruce can understand and fight for – even die for.

In the form of their adversary we see a caricature of a prodigal body, Edward Longshanks – 'the hammer of the Scots'. Edward sees life simply and brutally when he describes the Scottish question, "The trouble with Scotland is that it is full of Scots". This kind of physical deduction and solution is used time and time again to deal with his problems, whether it is about family or politics. He throws his son's friend to his death and calls for Wallace's capture with the words, "Bring me Wallace. Alive, if possible. Dead, just as good". When a commander reminds him that a command to unleash the archery will kill his own troops as well, he retorts 'that they will kill the enemy and there are plenty of English reserves'. His solutions in life have the same simple nature of the prodigal body, largely unfettered by the prodigal heart and completely uncomplicated by the prodigal mind – a true Brute.

In the following text the randomly chosen names of a number of celebrities have been arranged by the author into three groups. The reader is invited to decide which group of people best represents each prodigal type and to which group the reader might belong.

Group 1 – Tony Blair, Robbie Williams, George Bush junior, Robert Kilroy Silk (who started the political party, Veritas), Oliver Reed, Groucho Marx, Gordon Ramsay, John Major, David Icke, Lee Evans, John the Gospel author.

Group 2 – Stephen Fry, Princess Diana, Bob Geldof, Mother Teresa, Bill Clinton, Rowan Williams, John Lennon, the singer Madonna, Jack Straw, Sting.

Group 3 – Mel Gibson, John Prescott, Sandy Toksvig, Charlie Drake, Arnold Schwarzeneggar, Gerald Ford, Winston Churchill, Ronald Reagan, Jonathan Ross, Jeremy Clarkson.

Chapter Three

The Sower and the Soils

Jesus recognised these three prodigal forms in the **parable of the Sower**. It was the one parable that it is said that Jesus wanted people to most understand. It is also the only one that he attempted to explain. This suggests it had a difficult, but very important message. It held within it the Truth or 'seed'.

In this story Jesus talks of a man who goes out to sow seeds. The seed is the Trinity of the Father, Son and Holy Spirit – the concept of God's self within us. In the seed lies an embryonic plant which is used symbolically by Jesus to describe self. The shoot is symbolic of the heart, feeling or **Life**; the root of the mind, understanding or **Truth**; and the whole plant (unity) of the body, fellowship or **Way**. **See Figure 6 – The plant of the Kingdom.**

The seed is in effect the call to the prodigal Son for humility, the narrow gate into the Kingdom and so salvation. The seed meets three different soils which refer to the three different prodigal types. Each prodigal type produces a different response to the message. Each prodigal type or Son finds the Father within them as a Father of love and forgiveness – but is not 'born again in the spirit'. They do not find the Holy Spirit within themselves. The seed germinates but the plant dies. This is because the part of the plant that contains the Father and His will grows but the prodigal Son receives nothing of the Father's growth and his half of the plant does not grow, so the whole plant (Father and Son) withers.

FIGURE 6
The Kingdom as a plant

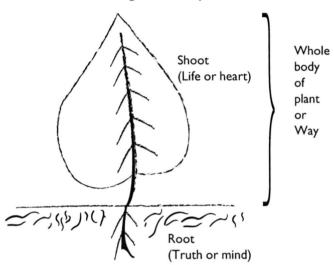

Shoot
(Life or heart)

Whole
body
of
plant
or
Way

Root
(Truth or mind)

The fourth soil is 'good' soil. The seed germinates, grows into a healthy plant and produces many seeds of its own. This is the person who finds the Father's self and His Love, the humility of the prodigal Son, and so the Helper or Holy Spirit also – all three persons of God's self within himself. The difference between himself and the other three is that he sees the 'narrow gate' of humility. He accepts as the prodigal Son the knowledge that he is bankrupt and has nothing to offer the Father in His Kingdom and so God's self – except his humility, freely given. He finds that this humility or will, freely given, is his share in the person of the Holy Spirit or Helper, with whom he is reunited in the Kingdom along with the Father's will, His love. He receives the help of the Father by the Holy Spirit and so his prodigal half of the plant grows and the whole plant prospers and is able to give help or produce seeds.

In the case of the other three soils, although they were aware of the Father within they were not joined in common will with the Father in the person of the Holy Spirit – and so received no help from the Helper and gave no help (produced no seeds).

The first soil is the stony ground. This is the soil represented by the Lucifer prodigal Son. The seed germinates a little root but no shoot, and the birds come and eat up the seed and carry it away. The part of the plant that is prodigal and not humble (understands its bankruptcy) will not grow. The part that is the Father's grows but is not sustained by the prodigal part and the whole plant (Father, Son and Holy Spirit) dies. **See Figure 7 – The seed of Lucifer**

In this case the birds come and take away the body or fellowship of the Father, where it lies dormant, before it has time to grow. These birds are the 'affairs' of the prodigal heart – the loves and passions of the heart that ensnare Lucifer.

The second soil is the shallow soil. This is the soil represented by the snake prodigal type. The seed germinates and the shoot grows fully. This person's heart is filled with great feelings of joy, gladness and love (Life). However the mind is prodigal (arrogant) and the root does not grow. It does not receive an understanding (Truth) of the Trinity from the Holy Spirit. The fellowship or body of the plant is half complete. When adversity (drought) comes the plant dies as there is insufficient root (and so nutrients and water) to support the shoot, the healthy part of the plant. The whole plant (Father, Son and Holy Spirit) dies. **See Figure 8 – The seed of the snake.**

The third soil is the deep soil. This is the soil represented by the Brute or prodigal body. The seed germinates and the root (mind) is filled with understanding (Truth) and it grows fully. The shoot (Life) half develops because there is a prodigal half to the heart. There is a prodigal body to the plant and so it is doomed. The cares and worries of the prodigal body and fellowship, in the form of thorns, grow up and choke the half formed shoot. The whole plant (Father, Son and Holy Spirit) dies. **See Figure 9 – The seed of the Brute.**

In each case the prodigal self has not acknowledged its own bankruptcy in the Son and so humility in the Holy Spirit. For this reason the Holy Spirit is unable to help the Son with the Father's wealth. So the Father, Son and Holy Spirit (whole plant) is lost.

FIGURE 7
The Seed of Lucifer (Stony ground)

Father body/half mind

Prodigal body/half mind

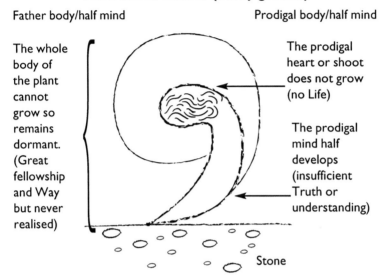

The whole body of the plant cannot grow so remains dormant. (Great fellowship and Way but never realised)

The prodigal heart or shoot does not grow (no Life)

The prodigal mind half develops (insufficient Truth or understanding)

Stone

FIGURE 8
The Seed of the Snake (shallow soil)

Father heart/half body

Prodigal mind/half body

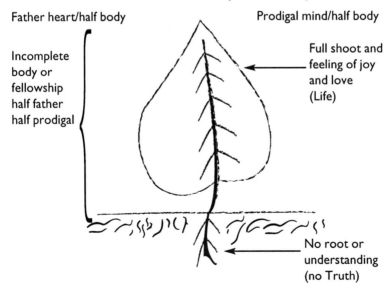

Incomplete body or fellowship half father half prodigal

Full shoot and feeling of joy and love (Life)

No root or understanding (no Truth)

The fourth soil is the 'good' soil where the prodigal Son accepts he is bankrupt. He has wasted all and can offer the Father nothing of what he has taken of his inheritance – only his spirit of Love (share in the person of the Holy Spirit). This love can only therefore take the form of self knowledge, an abject humility. The Father can then pour his love and wealth into the void of the prodigal Son in the form of his spirit of Love (share in the person of the Holy Spirit). The prodigal Son is born again by virtue of his own humility, the Father's generosity and both sharing in the help of the Holy Spirit. The prodigal part of this plant therefore prospers with the help of the Holy Spirit and Father's wealth. This plant (God's self) grows and matures and produces more seed which it sows or offers generously to others. **See Figure 10 – The seed of the humble prodigal Son.**

This prodigal Son's spirit of absolute humility, freely given, walks hand in hand with the Father's Spirit of absolute generosity by virtue of the person of the Holy Spirit. This is the grace that the prodigal self shares with others – the seed it sows.

It is this humble admission of bankruptcy, freely given, that opens the door to the Kingdom of Heaven. In essence it seems easy but in practice it is not. Jesus knows that the loss of innocence or Man's awareness of self opens him to the continual temptation to not see the prodigal self as 'bankrupt' – to be arrogant. Jesus says 'that the road to Salvation is narrow and few find it'.

The common experience of the Trinity, God's self or the Kingdom of Heaven and the road that leads to it, is expressed by Jesus in his parables. The parables that explain God's self begin with the words, "The Kingdom of Heaven is like . . . " In the parable of the vineyard, the owner goes out to the market place to hire people to work in it. He hires some people at the beginning of the day and they agree to be paid a pound for a day's work. He goes out again and hires more people and they agree the same wage – a pound. Some are hired at the last hour of the day and they agree the same wage – one pound. When the day is ended the workers are paid their wages and the workers who were hired at the beginning of the day grumble to the owner that they got the

FIGURE 9
The Seed of the Brute (deep soil)

Father mind/half heart   Prodigal body/half heart

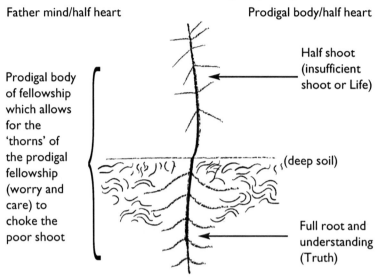

Half shoot (insufficient shoot or Life)

Prodigal body of fellowship which allows for the 'thorns' of the prodigal fellowship (worry and care) to choke the poor shoot

(deep soil)

Full root and understanding (Truth)

FIGURE 10
The Seed of the humble prodigal son (good soil)

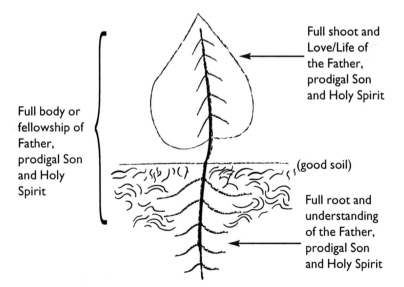

Full shoot and Love/Life of the Father, prodigal Son and Holy Spirit

Full body or fellowship of Father, prodigal Son and Holy Spirit

(good soil)

Full root and understanding of the Father, prodigal Son and Holy Spirit

same wage as those that worked barely an hour. The owner replied, "What are you complaining about? You agreed your wage as generous and fair. Why complain about my generosity to others". Here Jesus describes the nature of the grace in the Kingdom, when the prodigal Son (hired worker) agrees to work with the Father in His Kingdom. The prodigal Son's humility must be total and absolute, his commitment absolute. The response of the Father is also total kindness, absolute generosity of the Kingdom – eternal Life. The Father does not and cannot withhold Himself. The prodigal Son cannot offer a 'little' humility, for bankruptcy is a term that describes a total loss.

Jesus hints again at the absolute value and indivisibility of the Kingdom of Heaven – the commonality of God's self. Jesus sends out seventy followers to spread the message of the trinity or Kingdom within us. They return over excited and flying high with success. They talk of 'seeing Satan, the arrogant prodigal self or Son, crashing from the sky'. Jesus gently brings them to reality by saying, "Do not glory in the power but be thankful that your names are written in heaven". This is a poignant description of eternal life. It is not an eternal experience of prodigal self, bathing itself in glory forever. It is a sharing in a common sense of self or ownership in which people are only distinguished by their names – an ownership, or sense of separation within it, in name only.

This principle again is at the heart of the Beatitudes. Jesus calls all people who are finding their physical life hard and difficult, to be joyful and happy, for he had come to show something truly wonderful and rich beyond imagination, and that lay not outside them but within them – God's self.

Again he calls the weary and the down trodden to come to him for 'my burden is light and my yoke is easy'. It was a strange thing for someone like Jesus to say considering the beating he would receive, the cross he would carry and the death he would endure; He was not just talking the talk but walking the walk. He was saying that the salvation of the prodigal self or finding God's self within was worth any suffering or death of this world – for life was not life without it.

Chapter 4

The Original Sin

Just as Adam and Eve (symbolic of the first human) became aware of his inheritance as a Son and became prodigal, so every awakening child takes a prodigal self. Every child is born into a prodigal world of aware or prodigal humans. The child falls immediately to Temptation.

We may identify ourselves as a Lucifer, Snake or Brute form of the prodigal Son or divided self. There is a logic to which prodigal type we 'choose'. This process begins with the child being aware of itself with a Son's inheritance. It will also be aware of a half that belongs to a Father which is 'empty'. It will look to an earthly (and so prodigal) father figure to fill this void. It will choose that person who it believes to be 'in charge', the person upon whom its life depends. This is the 'key parent' and it may be male or female. The key parent, perceived by the child, may be the mother but often the mother will point the child to the father as the person in charge. In the case of Jesus, both his parents pointed to the Father in heaven as the Father of Jesus.

However here is a typical experience. If the father in a family is seen by the first child as the key parent or person in charge (or upon whom all life depends) this child will place the prodigal self of this father into his own Father half or self. If the father is a prodigal body (Brute), the first child will take the prodigal body and place it in its Father half. This will result in the child possessing the Lucifer form of the prodigal self or son. It is best described diagrammatically.

We can see some Truth in the saying, "The sins of the father are visited upon the son". The son looks to the father's prodigal self in order to 'choose' its own prodigal self. This is best described diagrammatically. **See Figure 11 – inheriting Lucifer**. This process is **completely** infallible. If the prodigal or earthly father is a Lucifer, the first child **will** be a snake. **See Figure 12 – inheriting the snake**. If the prodigal father is a snake then the first child **will** be a Brute. **See Figure 13 – inheriting the Brute**

This process of inheritance of the prodigal self continues with the second child and third and so on. The second child will respond to the elder sibling as the prodigal 'father' and respond accordingly. The third child will respond to the second sibling as their father. You will never see a family of three children without each being of different prodigal types.

An example is as follows. If there are two Brute parents the first child will be a Lucifer. The second child will be a snake and the third child will be a Brute.

There can be an anomaly to this 'clockwork' progression of inheritance. The middle child of a family (often the second of three children) may not follow the progression. It occurs when there is a strong Lucifer presence in the key parent or both parents, who produce a first child who is a snake (prodigal mind).The next child does not become a prodigal body but a Lucifer. The child seems to react to not just the key parent (the elder sibling) but the sensation of being at the heart of a prodigal fellowship or body. This sensation is exaggerated by two or one very strong Lucifer parents who always promote a very strong sense of prodigal fellowship in their marriages and family. The third child will then take up the missing prodigal type – the prodigal body. These Lucifers often have a sensation of being the 'odd one out'.

In the royal family we see Prince Charles, a prodigal mind, marry Princess Diana, also a prodigal mind. Either Charles or Diana may have been the key parent to the first child, Prince William, who is therefore a prodigal body. The second child,

FIGURE 11
Inheriting Lucifer

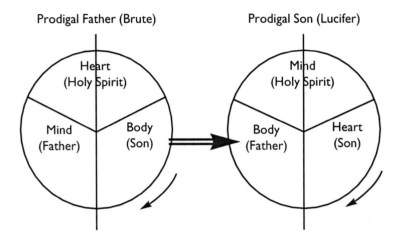

FIGURE 12
Inheriting the Snake

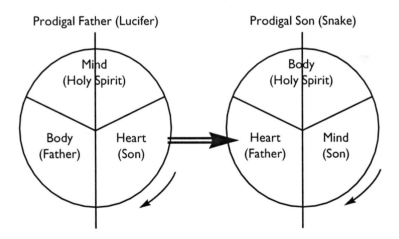

FIGURE 13
Inheriting the Brute

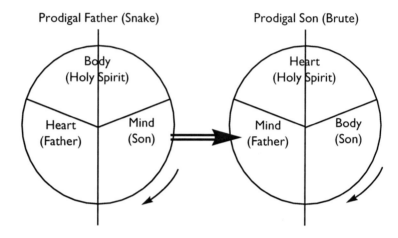

Prince Harry, responds to his elder brother's prodigal self and is a prodigal heart. If Charles and Diana had had a third child, this child would have been a prodigal mind.

It is important not to think the prodigal self loves the prodigal father. The prodigal Son may hate or fear the prodigal father and person of Love (his will). It will simply deem this person to be in charge of its life.

The machinations of this simple philosophy are as 'far reaching' as Life itself, affecting every aspect of our mental, emotional and physical existence – and Jesus knew it. It led him to hand out a warning about families with the words, "Your worst enemy is within your own household". We determine our prodigal selves and our imprisonment within them by virtue of our prodigal fathers or family.

When we familiarise ourselves with the nature of these three prodigal Sons and their prodigal fathers, it opens up a new world of understanding human behaviour. The behaviour of the prodigal Son is tragically predictable and ultimately always self destructive. Our prodigal self dooms us from birth. However Jesus shows the Father as a person to whom original sin (the irreversible sin of awareness) is not an obstacle to His love. He is a person who cannot return the prodigal Son to a pre-prodigal, unaware, sinless or innocent state but can offer all his resources to the Helper or Holy Spirit so that the prodigal self can survive and have the Kingdom or God's self. The Father is no longer of the Old Testament, a person who demands nothing but perfection of a 'sin free' Son, dishing out punishment and reward, revenge and mercy until He gets what He wants. He is not a Father who weighs up our good or bad points before he accepts or rejects us. He is a Father who wants to help us in a shared or common Spirit of free will. He wants us to be where we belong, in our Kingdom. He wants us to find the door of humility – by our own free will. He wants us, not Him, to be our judge.

Therefore the prodigal Son can be saved by help from the Holy Spirit, only by its own 'choice', by choosing to be helped, by his own humility. Just as we **unconsciously**, at birth, chose our prodigal father and so our prodigal self, we are given the power to **consciously** choose to reject our prodigal father and return to our common Father within. In doing so, we join in the shared spirit of Love or Holy Spirit and its help. One road leads unconsciously to a dead end prison of a prodigal self and the other consciously to the eternal freedom of God's self.

Chapter Five

Salvation and the Eye of a Needle

Salvation and the eye of a needle

The definition of salvation to Jesus was not the eradication of the awareness or knowledge that Adam and Eve had stolen for themselves, which was not possible. Salvation for the prodigal self was not even finding the Father – but finding the Helper and so sharing in the help of the Father. In the parable of the Sower all three prodigal Sons or selves found the Father but not the Helper or Holy Spirit – grace. They did not find Salvation and could not offer it to others. They sowed no seeds. Indeed the Father could not survive in them and withered. They failed to find something, because it is where they are least likely to find it – within the self of the prodigal Son himself.

Jesus tells us that the road to the Kingdom, salvation, grace or the Helper is 'strait' or narrow – a narrow gate. "Strait is the gate and few find it". This symbol of the narrow gate belies a 'riddle'. It implies something that is simple, almost so simple and insignificant that it is easily overlooked. It does not entail something that involves great works, a great morality or goodness, complicated instructions, great intellect, years of learning or reading or even a great sacrifice or love (worship). Jesus actually said he did not want sacrifice or 'payment'. It is not something we can buy with even our own blood. This narrow gate implies that it is not something we do but something we do not do. In fact it is something we must stop doing. We have to find or strike an attitude – of absolute humility. We have to stop believing we have something to offer – stop being arrogant. We are in every way possible, 'bankrupt'.

Humility is not an abrogation of the prodigal self – an eternal state of feeling sorry or guilty about the Original Sin and the prodigal self. It is knowledge (in the mind, heart, body and soul or being) of what the prodigal self is. The prodigal Son is the son who ate of the tree of knowledge and so became aware and therefore prodigal or separated from the Father or the innocent grace with Him. The prodigal Son's will separates from the Father's will.

See Figure 14 – The separation of the will of the Father and prodigal son in the Holy Spirit

Humility is the realisation or knowledge that the prodigal Son is 'bankrupt'. For all he has gained by awareness in terms of discovering the self of the son, and for all his will in the Holy Spirit, he is powerless and bankrupt without the Father and His

FIGURE 14
The separation of the Father and Son's will in the Holy Spirit
Holy Spirit or Helper

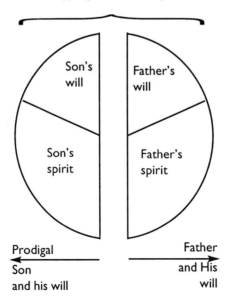

Son's
will

Father's
will

Son's
spirit

Father's
spirit

Prodigal
Son
and his will

Father
and His
will

will in the Holy Spirit. He needs his Father's half to give him a true sense of self – God's self or the Kingdom.

Jesus describes this 'gate' or humility as that possessed by a child. He said a person cannot enter the Kingdom of Heaven (the common self) without first becoming as a child. This is not a reference to the 'innocence' of a child, but actually the opposite – the knowledge of the child. The child is not sorry for being a child or guilty about itself. It does not seek any arrogant illusions of its own independence. The child's humility lies in its knowledge of what it is – a being that cannot exist without a father and his help. It cannot go it alone and it puts its hand into the hand of its father, albeit a prodigal one, and walks with the father – asking and accepting his help with complete trust. Father and son voluntarily join their wills.

Jesus also describes the Kingdom of Heaven for the prodigal Son as a master to servant relationship. In order for the servant (prodigal Son) to be a 'good' servant, the master (the Father) shares all he has with the servant, so that servant can serve him with it. The servant in turn glorifies the master by serving the master with all his loyalty and will. They can act as one by virtue of their common will alone. The child is protected or helped by its father by virtue of its own willingness to be helped – the child's own will. The servant is a 'good' servant by virtue of his own free will. The prodigal or bankrupt Son is saved by virtue of his own will – not the mercy of the Father, but their common love in the Holy Spirit.

Jesus tells a number of parables to emphasise the importance of seeing humility as a free will, desire or love. "Seek and ye shall find. Knock and the door shall be opened." If we want then we ask. If we do not ask therefore, then how can it be given? Jesus tells of a story of a man who finds a treasure and rushes away and sells all that he has so that he can buy the field where the treasure lies. Salvation is a treasure that is worth as much as all the physical creation – it is priceless. We have to want it as much as all there is in creation – therefore we must put a price on it beyond anything within creation. This will or desire must be unfailing just as the Father's will or desire to love is unfailing. Jesus tells another story to illustrate this persistence. A widow demands her rights from a local judge. She pesters the judge night and day until the judge gives her what she **wants** just in order to get rid of her and get a good night's sleep. Jesus says, 'If a bad uncaring judge gives this person her rights, then can you imagine a good judge (the Father) refusing this widow her rights?' Jesus is saying that all people have the Kingdom of Heaven within them – the persons of the prodigal Son, the Father and the common person of Love or Helper. It is therefore our right to have it, if we want it.

Jesus also told a number of parables that warned people that the desire or will of the prodigal Son had to be perpetually 'awake' or watchful. "Be dressed ready for service and keep your lamps burning, like men waiting for their master to return from a wedding banquet, so that when he comes and knocks, they can open the door immediately and let him in". Here Jesus is saying that the prodigal Son has a share in and so a part to play in the person of the Holy Spirit. He has a responsibility in his own grace – one of receiving. If we are not awake to receive, then we cannot receive. Our grace or help is not just to serve us but is something that we are asked to serve with. The same sentiment is expressed in the **parable of the Ten Virgins** with their oil lamps. Jesus is explaining that the prodigal Son's undoing was the act of becoming aware or conscious to himself and his 'inheritance'. His responsibility and help now lie in that very consciousness. He must employ that very consciousness to become aware of the Trinity, and so find grace. He must be forever dressed for service – and awake. This was an important message for the disciples to absorb upon whom Jesus knew everything would depend when he was physically gone.

Before Jesus, people devoid of the 'knowledge' of the Kingdom, felt abandoned and alone, and judged the presence or absence of God in their lives according to what happened to them. Jesus wanted people to stop this. "Do not judge by external standards but by internal standards". He asked people to judge the presence of God not by what happened outside them but by the presence or absence of God's self (the Kingdom) **within** them. God's wealth (in mind, heart and body) and so grace came from within.

A tower had fallen on people in Siloam and killed eighteen people. Those who survived were deemed to have been favoured by God, and those that died to be punished by God. Jesus used this event to denounce such an attitude. God favoured and punished no-one. All events were natural happenings (even when man-made) and were not used by God to favour or punish anyone. God is a God of Love who seeks only to help. Instead he asked people to consider the state of their own relationship with the Kingdom. Were they all not guilty of Original Sin? Was not everyone, dead and alive, guilty of a lack of humility? Was not everyone a failure in this? Did anyone love his enemy as himself? Give to all who ask? Lend without any thought of return? Do good to those that harm them? Were not all equally guilty, even those who were not killed by the falling tower? Are we not our worst enemy? Do we not in fact punish and condemn ourselves?

A lack of humility is the message also buried in the **parable of the Talents**. It is the reason for the failure of the servant to invest his talent. A master (The Father) goes away and leaves money with his three servants (symbolic of the prodigal Sons). To one he gives ten talents, to another five and to the last servant, just one. He returns and asks the servants to give an account of his money. The servants who had been given ten and five talents had both gone out and invested the money and made a return or profit. The one who had one talent had hidden the money for safe keeping. He handed the talent back to the master saying, "I knew you were a hard master and could see that you reaped where you do not sow, so I thought it best if I kept your money safe". The master was angry and took the talent off him and gave it to the servant who had the ten talents and had made the most money. He dismissed his 'wicked' servant. This servant was judged not for his cowardice but for judging the master by external standards. He had judged the master to be a cruel and unloving person by the fact that he seemed to punish people for not having talents, who it appeared had been given none in the first place. The talent is the 'knowledge of the Kingdom'. He seemed therefore to punish the innocent – those without knowledge. He had not realised that all people were not innocent but guilty. He had been given, just by the master's generosity, a talent (the knowledge) not for his own salvation but for the salvation of others. The master gave the talent (knowledge) to the servant so he could multiply it for him (save others) – not just save himself. He had judged the master (Father) by external standards, by what he thought the Father was doing outside him, not internal standards and by what the Father wished to do from within him.

Jesus warns people to look for and foster the God within, not outside, ourselves. He asks people not to worry about what they are going to wear or to eat – the most essential necessities of life. "Life is more than food, the body more than clothes". He says that worry destroys grace, by which all these things come to us. He is not suggesting that people do not work, but that we do not worry. Be ambivalent towards these things.

Jesus in the Beatitudes actually blesses those who are meek and humble – people who know they have nothing to offer to the Kingdom. He calls them blessed and says they shall inherit the earth. They will rule for they will inherit grace in God. They have the knowledge of the Father, Son and Holy Spirit within. These are the people who know that they need the wealth of the Father and so will receive it. So he also blesses the poor in spirit (humble in soul), those that hunger for righteousness and justice (humble in mind), those that mourn (humble in fellowship), those that are pure in heart (humble of heart). All these people will, because of their humility, receive what they yearn for.

Jesus makes another reference to the fact that God as the Trinity of persons is within us – and we will not find Him outside us. He tells a story of a master (God) who builds a vineyard (the world). He builds a wall around it and goes away. He leaves people as stewards (Man in His own image) to tend it and deliver to Him a harvest (a reflection of Himself). The stewards forget who and what they are. The master sends one or two of his servants (prophets) to remind people that they are in His image and are expected to deliver a harvest. They are blind to this knowledge and beat them up and do not listen. He then decides to send His own son (Jesus) who fully understands the image of God (the Trinity within) and they beat him up and kill him. In Jesus people fail to recognise the Trinity or Kingdom within them and the narrow gate to it – humility. They do not see the will of God and the harvest expected of them. In this story God the Father has created this world, as it is, and gone away. He only appears as a spirit within people offering grace with this pre-ordained world. He does not intervene as some supernatural person outside people to change His own world, His own nature.

So Jesus is not some supernatural being but a prodigal person born into a prodigal world. He has no special power over the world. He struggles with his prodigal self as we all do. He stumbles, agonises, suffers temptation and self doubt – but we see him always redeemed by his commitment to his own humility. His own humility as a prodigal self restores his belief, faith and strength over and over again right up to the end – and gives him grace. Jesus calls this humility (or knowledge of our bankruptcy or common guilt of Original Sin) the key to the Kingdom of Heaven.

Out of the historical literature of Christianity has evolved the story of the **Holy Grail** – a mystical relic that symbolises the material proof, and so the power, of Jesus as God. It is the Christian equivalent of a talisman. It is mooted to be many different artefacts – the wine cup from the last supper, Jesus' blood line with Mary Magdalene, the womb of Mary Magdalene, John the Baptist's head, the heart of Jesus and so on. The supposed hiding places of this Grail are similarly hazy and numerous. One thing is for sure, the Holy Grail will remain a mystery.

This Grail is a symbol of what gave power to Jesus the man – what gave him grace with God. It is a symbol of his knowledge (Truth), love (Life) and body (Way). It is suggested this artefact contains this power....and so the search goes on.

This story, in a perverse way, describes well the riddle of Jesus' power – humility. He knew the prodigal Son, Father and Holy Spirit (their common wills) lay within. He knew only the humility (knowledge of his own bankruptcy) of the prodigal Son was the key to grace with the Father and His love in the person of the Holy Spirit. This knowledge or humility lies only in our personal choice or free will and cannot be found outside us and so can never be symbolised by anything material.

Jesus left behind no symbol or talisman. He left only an example of his own absolute humility. His death on a cross is the enduring example of the humility that is asked of every prodigal Son – that every person, as a prodigal self, has to face the reality that they personally are wholly responsible for all the sins of the world (past, present and future) and show the appropriate humility and forgiveness. The power to do this lies not in any help of a talisman outside us but in the power of the Trinity of persons, Kingdom or God's self within us.

Chapter Six

All Things are Possible with God

These words are probably the most loaded ever uttered by Jesus – and the most commonly taken out of context and so misunderstood.

This statement was not some grandiose gesture to give people hope, faith and trust or inspire people in yet another religion. They were words designed to precisely define the nature of self in Man – the Trinity of Father, Son and Holy Spirit. To Jesus belief was not a hope but a precise **knowledge**. Faith was following with the heart a complete certainty. Trust was the unquestioning reliance on firm ground, something we know is solid and real.

Jesus is telling us to have belief, faith and trust in the Trinity of self within – God the Father, Son and Holy Spirit. As prodigal or aware Sons we can have absolute certainty of the love of God the Father through the Holy Spirit (the Helper), if we remain humble. God the Father's will, in the Holy Spirit, is only to love. However God the Father is infinite and we cannot set any limits on Him. He is boundless in His wealth and what He can and does offer freely in the person of the Holy Spirit. He transcends all form and structure. Jesus describes this with the words, "No man can look upon the face of God". It follows therefore that God's self, the Trinity of persons, our own sense of self, God's help or grace are all boundless. All things therefore are possible with God.

Jesus is setting into Man a self that transcends all form or structure – an invitation not to define or limit self and therefore ourselves. This actually goes against our very own instincts of a sense of self as something that **gives** us boundaries and walls, a zone of familiarity and comfort. This also undermined the theocracy or religious authorities whose whole role was to define God for the people and impress a social order with their definitions. Jesus threw fuel onto the fire when he defined the fellowship of his 'church' with the words, "When two or more are gathered in my name, I shall be there and whatever you ask for will be granted". He is giving anyone the authority to call upon the Holy Spirit, in the most minimal fellowship, for help – which will be granted.

Jesus is not defining the Holy Spirit as a person who bows to the wishes of the prodigal Son – a Father Christmas figure. He is defining the Spirit as a person of which the prodigal Son's will is a part, and which has no bounds. This person speaks and does for itself and has a name. Jesus makes this point when he says his followers must remain, 'a part of the vine'. This vine is this person or sense of self. If a branch comes off the vine it withers. The prodigal self stays in the vine by realising that he is a part of the vine; it is his inheritance whether bankrupt or not. His humility is his generosity that makes him part of the vine – and keeps him part of it.

Jesus always identifies with the person of the Holy Spirit, the vine. In the garden of Gethsemane Jesus accepts that his own approaching torture and death are in the interests of the revelation and glorification of the Trinity, the Father and Holy Spirit – and so in the prodigal Son's interest too. Despite all his personal suffering Jesus is taken care of and given the strength to proceed to his goal. His sacrifice is not some compliance with fate but his own will (and the Father's) in this person of free wills. He reminds his disciples constantly that although 'All things are possible with God' this is an agreed action of God. Jesus is fully informed and knows what he is doing and why – by virtue of the Holy Spirit. This why Christians see the figure of Jesus on the cross as a deliberate conspiratorial act by God the Father, God the Son and God the Holy Spirit. Jesus as a prodigal Son, by virtue of his own humility, faces up to his full responsibility (guilt) for the Original Sin (all the sin in the world) and so is joined in grace on the cross with the Father and Holy Spirit. The cross is therefore an invitation for all prodigal selves or Sons to also carry the full responsibility or cross.

Although God is limitless and makes all things possible, it does not mean that God is anarchic. God's spirit obeys its own rules. At the moment of Jesus' baptism by John, he was born again and realised the presence of God's self or Trinity within. The words, "This is my son, with whom I am well pleased" is an indication of Jesus as a prodigal self finding the acceptance of the Father within. He is accepted and loved as he is – bankrupt or not. The 'dove' of the Holy Spirit descends upon him as Jesus realises that the person of the Holy Spirit is the shared will of the Father and Son (however prodigal). Jesus now had to determine what this 'born again' experience or revelation of God's self within himself (and so all people) meant. How does God's self dwell within Man? What is the power of the Trinity? Jesus was troubled with doubts and confusion.

Jesus took himself off into the wilderness to be alone and struggle with this revelation – to define it. The arrogant prodigal self as Satan was not going to let Jesus go that easily.

In the **first Temptation** Satan in the form of the prodigal mind or **snake** challenges the mind of the Son within the Trinity. What can it do that the prodigal mind cannot? The prodigal mind or snake challenges Jesus to turn the stones into bread. Jesus replies that he cannot. Instead he tells the prodigal mind that "Man cannot live on bread alone, but on every word from the mouth of God". The mind of God, the Trinity, is open to all possibilities and realities in God's creation – that is its power. It does not give the power to change the creation, but grace to see all the creation and 'what it is doing'. Later Jesus demonstrates the power of the mind of God or Trinity– the power of **knowledge, conviction or belief**. In the **miracle of the wine** in Cana, the guests experience water served to them as wine. Jesus plants the idea and the guests allow Jesus to seed the idea into their selves, that the water that has been served is in fact wine. They not only experience it is wine, but the best wine of the evening. Jesus demonstrates that it is the sense of self that dictates or serves us with what we believe or 'know' and it is that belief that serves us with its reality. The prodigal person is served with the belief of the prodigal self and therefore the prodigal reality. The person of the Trinity is served with the belief or knowledge of the Trinity and the reality (every word from the mouth of God) of the Trinity. Seeing is believing or having knowledge and it is what the self allows into it that dictates what it sees – not the other way around.

In the **second Temptation** Satan in the form of **Lucifer** or the arrogant prodigal heart challenges the heart of the Trinity. What can it do that the prodigal heart cannot? The prodigal heart or Lucifer challenges Jesus to throw himself off the Temple roof. And if he has any credibility as the Son of God, he will not be killed. Jesus replies that he cannot with the words, "Do not tempt the Lord thy God". Jesus is saying that God does not intervene physically in the creation and we cannot tempt Him to do so. The power of the heart of the Trinity lies in **intuitive knowledge** – responding to all the opportunities that creation provides – with which to support and save ourselves. Later Jesus demonstrates the power of the heart of God or Trinity (intuition) by taking advantage of a natural opportunity to walk or 'sail' on water. Jesus did not weigh up and study all the prevalent wind and water conditions around him but responded to a 'feeling' from the heart (the heart of God within) that the conditions were perfect for his 'walk'.

In the **third Temptation** Satan in the form of the arrogant prodigal body or **Brute** challenges the body or fellowship of the Trinity or God's self. What can the body or fellowship of the Trinity do that the prodigal body cannot? Satan takes Jesus to a high point and shows him the world, its material wealth. He tells Jesus that he can have anything he wants, if he will only bow down, worship or work for him. Jesus refuses Satan's offer and puts his trust in the help of the Trinity or God's self to provide what it desires for him. Later Jesus reveals the power or **grace** of the fellowship of the Trinity in the miracle of the **feeding of the 5000**. A large crowd had come to hear him speak from miles around. Afterwards it was obvious that they were hungry and in need of food. Jesus made the disciples go out and split them into rows of fifty people. The disciples beckoned a boy to Jesus who had a basket of 5 loaves and 2 fishes. He split the food into baskets, one for each row. This basket was then passed down the line of each row. As it passed down the line, those that were hungry took food and those that had a surplus of food donated what they didn't need to the basket. When the baskets came to the end of the rows they were filled with food. Jesus demonstrated that the spirit of sharing and unity (the fellowship of God's self) provides Man with more than he needs. There are further instances where Jesus demonstrates how the power of the fellowship of the Trinity (God's self within) provides us with what we need.

Jesus now has defined God's self as a Trinity of persons – the Father, Son and Holy Spirit (the shared wills of Father and Son). He has established that it is the will of the Father to offer the prodigal Son all that He has in response to the prodigal Son offering all that he has to the Father – which is only his own will (for he is bankrupt and has nothing else). This comes in the form of the shared person of the Holy Spirit as help. The prodigal Son therefore shares and is involved fully in this process of grace or help – he is invited to place himself in a position where he can receive help.

Jesus defines salvation as the Helper – being helped and helping, for the sake of the Kingdom, Trinity or God's self. The Father does not interfere with the life of the prodigal Son but invites him into a mutually beneficial relationship – like master and servant. Often the help from the Father that is given is purposefully small but invites a big response from the Son, so glorifying the Son. Often the help from the Father is great and invites a small response of the Son so glorifying the Father. A small gift from either Father or Son can, at the right moment, be magnified to make a great difference and this is the power of grace. This is the lesson behind the **story of the Good Samaritan** – how a very small helping hand in the right way, at the right time, and accepted fully can make a great difference to a life. It is like a small seed that grows into something far bigger than its original self – the seed being a favourite analogy of Jesus'. This is the role of the Helper or Holy Spirit – to know precisely what is helpful.

It was with this spirit of helpfulness that Jesus blessed the future church. He grants to Peter the 'keys to the Kingdom of Heaven' – an extraordinary gesture of trust. He is granting Man the power and responsibility of the Holy Spirit – to love, forgive, regenerate and make new in the name or Spirit of the Helper. He is giving to Man collectively the power, authority and permission to define or decide what is good for Man – what best reconciles the prodigal Son with the Father in terms of his own fellowship. He tells Peter, "What you bind (command) on earth, you bind in heaven, and what you loose (permit) on earth, will be loosed in heaven". Jesus defines the Holy Spirit as the Helper and asks the authority of the church to be generous, gentle, forgiving, loving and helpful as the Helper.

Jesus goes further than this in telling the disciples as founders of his church that they are 'custodians of a house and they must bring out of the storeroom old and new truths'. He is warning them not to be inflexible but creative, like the Holy Spirit. Man's relationship, as the 'aware' prodigal Son, with the Father has to be a dynamic relationship, something that evolves and changes. The Father cannot strip the prodigal Son of his awareness but has elected to forgive him and work with him. Jesus says that we must accept and give to Caesar or the prodigal world, just as God gives. The expression of the Truth of God's self or Trinity within Man cannot be followed as instructions from a book but as a Spirit or person – which is what it is. The expression of the Holy Spirit changes from culture to culture, century to century, person to person. An expression or interpretation of the Truth may be appropriate in one age and not in another, in one culture but not in another. What is helpful to one person may be counter productive in another. It is important for the Holy Spirit to be allowed to express itself (grace and love) in the 'language' and form that is appropriate to the age, person and culture.

Jesus described the presence of the Trinity within Man as a 'peace and love that passes all understanding'. This may seem at odds with Jesus as he agonises and sweats blood in the garden. But Jesus is not saying that maintaining this presence of the Kingdom within is easy. It requires an effort. However its presence is a peace. The prodigal self outside the Kingdom (off the vine) lives without the certainty, feeling and security that he is not alone. He does not see the Helper and lives without His knowledge and help. He cannot experience belief, faith and trust, because he has no 'knowledge' or certainty in which to practice belief, faith and trust. With certainty or knowledge comes authority and Jesus was described as a 'man of authority'.

The miracles are manifestations of this authority, of how the Father helps the prodigal Son in the common person of the Holy Spirit or common will. Miracles are defined as 'acts of wonder', help or grace and are not therefore supernatural acts or magic as they have come to be seen. His followers are tempted to see them as powerful supernatural acts, the significance of which as acts of humility and grace was initially lost on them. Jesus assured them that they were manifestations of the natural world by saying, "I only do what I see the Father doing". He is only seeing, feeling and acting upon natural opportunities. There is a reference in Mark's gospel to Jesus being 'dismayed that they (the disciples) had not understood the real meaning of the feeding of the five thousand. Their minds could not grasp it'. They no doubt saw the food appearing as magic out of thin air, rather than as a result of the generosity and help of the Holy Spirit within Man.

The miracle of the wine – a lesson in belief

Here Jesus is invited to a wedding in Cana. Some disciples and his mother are present. The wine runs out and his mother asks her son for help. Jesus rebukes her and says, "You must not tell me what to do, my time has not yet come". Here he is reminding his mother of his authority and what is left of his life is his own. He is not beholden to even his mother – only to God. In such times a Jewish man would have not talked to his mother in these terms. His mother respects this and says to a servant, "Do whatever he tells you".

Jesus tells the servants to fill six stone jars with water. He asks them to draw out some water and take it to the man in charge of the feast. This would have been poured into his earthenware goblet. The host would have had absolutely no reason to believe that he was drinking anything other than wine. The host was impressed and announced to the guests that the best wine had been kept to the end. The wine was then poured out for everyone else and they would have all had no reason to doubt their host. The watching disciples and servants who knew the pitchers were full of water were amazed.

The goblets may have had traces of wine present in them. Everyone may have been a little tipsy. It may have been dark. However the real reason that people tasted wine rather than water was their conviction or belief that it was wine. Jesus had planted the idea into the host and the host into his guests. If an idea is planted into the self with sufficient authority for it to be accepted, then the planted idea will serve that self with its belief (not the other way around as expected). That person's belief will then serve its own reality – in this case the person will taste the flavour of wine.

Jesus is making the important point that reality is a consequence of a belief or conviction and belief is a consequence of what idea or spirit we have within or allow into ourselves. We cannot just believe in the Kingdom, we have to allow the spirit of the Kingdom into our selves so that it can serve us with its belief or certainty – and so its reality. Belief is the mind's response to certainty or knowledge within us. Although we cannot change water into wine or stones into bread we can find the reality of wine and bread within us.

The miracle of walking on water – a lesson in faith

Jesus was sad at the death of John the Baptist and feeling disheartened and alone. He wanted time on his own. While he said goodbye to the people, Jesus asked his disciples to get into their boat and go ahead of him to Bethsiada. He went onto a hill to pray. He saw his disciples struggling against the wind in the middle of the lake; 'they were straining at the oars'. They were about three miles out. Jesus watched and then walked slowly to the water's edge. The Holy Spirit (his intuition) guided him to venture onto the water. He raised his robed arms and launched himself onto the water. The wind caught him and buoyed him up as he waded in the favourable currents. He was gaining fast on the boat after four or five 'tacks' into the wind. The disciples spotted him and thinking he was a ghost dropped their oars and started shouting at him. He realised he had frightened them and shouted that they must not be afraid, as he thought they might upset the boat. He tacked again and so 'looked as if he was going to pass them'. Jesus knew that he had little time left as the conditions were changing. He moved alongside the boat and climbed in, 'just as the wind died down'. So Jesus was using a condition of the wind and waves as sail boarders and boats do.

The disciples were completely amazed because they thought he had done something supernatural rather than just used the natural, if unusual, wind and water conditions. Jesus realised this and it was at this point he was dismayed that his disciples had not 'understood the feeding of the 5000'. They saw the miracles as supernatural, and so learned nothing from them.

They were then able to proceed easily to Bethsaida by oar for the wind had died down. Here Jesus was showing the disciples that although we cannot change the physical events of creation (or tempt them to change), we can be helped by them if we have the full presence of God within us. Faith is not blind but the heart's response to a certainty, a knowledge within.

The miracle of the feeding of the 5000 – a lesson in trust

Jesus and his disciples had been teaching and healing the sick. They were all tired and hungry. Also Jesus was saddened about John the Baptist's death. He was so indebted to him and later met and talked to his spirit during the Transfiguration. Jesus told his disciples he wanted to go to a lonely place and rest. They started off in a boat for such a place. By now however Jesus was well known as the potential Messiah with God-given powers of healing, authority and wisdom. People were desperate for a liberator and leader, not least to free them from the Romans. They looked always in hope for the prophecy of the Messiah to come true – someone like Jesus. Word was out that Jesus was the one. They saw him leaving the boat and ran from town to town along the shore, telling people he was around. They ran excitedly from their houses and work places, grabbing food quickly as they went. It was customary for crowds to gather and listen to teachers in the open air as a past time – and it was customary to bring a picnic. So when Jesus beached the boat, he was greeted with a mob, 5000 strong not including women and children. Jesus was filled with tears when he saw how expectant they were, how lost they were. He chose a suitable spot with good acoustics and got his followers to sit them down. He began to teach them. Despite being tired, so charismatic, inspirational and authoritative was his teaching that when he had finished the crowds made 'as if to rush him and proclaim him their leader'.

It was getting late and the crowd were high and hungry. The disciples were keen to get the fidgety crowd on their way and suggested to Jesus they send them away to get some food anywhere they could find some – and so leave Jesus and themselves in peace. Jesus was irritated by his disciples' fear of the crowd and so lack of concern and suggested they sort out some food for the crowd. "What" they exclaimed, "It will cost us 200 silver coins!" They were suggesting it would bankrupt them. But Jesus was just testing them, finding out if they understood the power of the Holy Spirit or Helper. Jesus had been looking into the crowd and had seen people with food and so asked the disciples to go in search of some food. They asked around and found only a boy with a basket of 5 loaves and 2 fishes willing to admit he had brought food with him. Most people shrank back and shook their heads, denying they had any food. The disciples returned with the boy and said, "This is all there is, Lord". They were a little nervous of Jesus' enterprise, not understanding how a few morsels of food could pacify and satisfy a restless crowd. If anything they would create disappointment and unrest.

Jesus took the food, prayed and blessed it. He told the disciples and associates to divide the people into groups of hundreds and fifties and sit them in rows. He made them appoint a leader in each group. He then divided the food and gave it to the associates to hand on to each leader. The group leaders placed the food in a basket and asked everyone to remove what they wanted. As the basket travelled down the line, people placed into the basket food they had brought but did not need to give to those that had none. At the end of the exercise the baskets were overflowing with food and the crowd were all fed. Jesus asked for surplus food not to be wasted and given to the needy in the area. This was because the surplus food signified not just the generosity of the people but God's generosity.

Jesus demonstrated that the generosity of the fellowship (body) of the God the Trinity which exists in all people provides for all our needs. There is more than enough for all people if everyone trusts the generosity of the Trinity and its ability to provide us with all we need. Here Jesus is defining trust as not some childish naivety but the body/fellowship's response to a certainty – the generosity and wealth of the Trinity and its ability to sustain everyone.

The story of the mustard seed – a lesson in grace

The disciples (probably the prodigal heart Peter) ask Jesus how they can increase their faith. They are enthralled by Jesus' miracles and authority and want to be like him. Jesus' reply is not what they expected. He says, "If you have faith as much as a mustard seed you could say to that mountain, cast thyself into the sea, and it shall be done". The mustard seed is the smallest of seeds and yet grows into a tree and birds can nest in its braches.

Here Jesus is reiterating what he has indicated in all his teachings and miracles. Belief, faith and trust all come from within and are served by a knowledge of what we are. We **are** the Father, Son and Holy Spirit, in that these three persons are within us. If we acknowledge the Trinity within us, then and then only, can we have belief, faith and trust in it! Only then can we have the help or grace that comes with it – and so know what it knows. We cannot have belief, faith and trust in something we are not already certain and have knowledge of.

The mustard seed is not aware and has no prodigal self and so no capacity for self deception. It **has** no blindness or illusions as to what it is or what it will grow into. It has all the ingredients for growing into a tree already within it. It simply allows carbon dioxide, water, warmth and sunlight to enter it. The growth is done for it. It allows the tree to grow from it. Jesus is telling them that everyone has the Trinity already within them; the Truth, Life and Way; the Father, Son and Holy Spirit. It is the act of acknowledging God's self within them or the act of 'being born again' that will serve them with all the belief, faith and trust they will need, 'all that the Father has' – vision, intuition and trust.

Jesus is describing the nature of grace when he says, "You could say to that mountain, cast thyself into the sea and it shall be done". He is not saying this as an 'arrogant temptation of God' to do something for us, change His creation for us (as Lucifer goads Jesus to do in the second Temptation). He is saying that God's self within will serve us with the vision, intuition and instinct to **know** that the mountain is to be cast into the sea by God (a natural event). This is the potential power of grace – the knowledge of 'what the Father is doing'. We can know such an event is taking place and choose to be a part of it. We can go to the cliff and at the moment we know it is going to be thrown into the sea, command it. Grace gives the appearance that we have the power so it amazes only those without such grace. Jesus amazed such people.

A cursing of the fig tree – a lesson in prayer

As Jesus was walking with the disciples to Jerusalem he saw a fig tree in the distance. On closer inspection he found there were no figs on it as 'it was not the time for figs'. Jesus cursed the tree and said to it, "No one shall eat figs from you again". After returning the next day to Bethany the disciples noticed the tree was dead right to the roots. Jesus said 'when people pray and ask for something, they must believe that they have already received it and they will be given whatever they ask for'. He also said that when a person prays they must first forgive anything they have against anyone, so the Father will forgive the wrongs they have done.

Jesus again is describing prayer as a state of grace – a knowledge of what the Father is doing but also what he wants from us. Belief is a knowledge of this in the mind, intuition in the heart and instinct in the body/fellowship. But grace is only granted, whether it is a knowledge of what the Father is doing or what there is for us, when we are completely humble and so forgiving. It is given only to those who truly take their personal and whole responsibility for all the sins of the world. For that is all we can give, as prodigal Sons, in return for the total generosity of the Father – and so grace.

Jesus is seen teaching grace as he passes the fig tree. The tree takes Jesus' interest. He looks for figs that he knows will not be there, for they are not in season. He also 'knows' that the fig tree is sick and dying and, using the excuse he is upset that the fig tree has no fruit, he commands it to die. The disciples are amazed when they pass the tree and find it is 'withered to the roots'. The tree has appeared to have responded to Jesus' command (curse). It was in fact Jesus who responded to the knowledge that the tree was dying (in such a dry, harsh environment a sick tree will wither very quickly indeed). Jesus is not fooling with the disciples but making an important point. **Knowledge, whether as belief, intuition or instinct is power.** This is the argument with which he defeated Satan, in all his forms, during his Temptations in the wilderness. He presents the knowledge he has as a 'power of command' to illustrate this point. Knowledge is how the prodigal Son shares in the wealth and power of the Father – and the key is his own humility in the Holy Spirit.

In the **parable of the Talents** Jesus warns what happens to people if they do not share their grace or knowledge with others. Jesus forgives those who go against him because 'they know not what they do'. But he is less forgiving to those who 'know and are free in the Holy Spirit' but do nothing about it. They know what they are doing and are therefore traitors as far as the church is concerned. Paul warns people that they can blaspheme against, or disbelieve, the Father and the Son but not the Holy Spirit. To sin against, threaten, betray or blaspheme against the Holy Spirit is not forgivable and is a declaration of war against the church.

The calming of the storm – a lesson in overcoming adversity

In the miracle of the calming of the storm Jesus reveals how grace protects us. The presence of the Kingdom within us, the full mind, heart and body of God, can save us from our own prodigal selves – and others'.

In Jesus' day there were no rescue helicopters or G.P.S. and a storm often meant death and something to greatly fear. Jesus had preached all day and was tired and wanted to get some peace. He suggested to the disciples that they go across the lake by boat. The disciples climbed into the boat in which Jesus was already sitting. Other boats were there too, so obviously there was no hint of a storm. Lake Galilee is a small lake and is subject to fierce and unexpected squalls. Suddenly, and shortly after setting sail, a strong wind blew up. This was not a storm a long time coming but a ferocious squall, which disappear as fast as they appear. Jesus was sleeping in the back with his head on a pillow. The disciples panicked as water splashed over the sides of the boat and they were thrown violently around. There was no mention of rain. Such violence, when we find ourselves in the middle of it, is frightening irrespective of how short lived it may be.

The disciple woke Jesus who sat up and looked around. He would have seen pandemonium. A capsized boat meant almost certain death in those days. He stood aside from the mayhem and said, "Be quiet, be still!" Almost immediately the wind died down and the squall passed and there was a great calm. Jesus was showing absolutely no fear during the whole event. This would have shocked the people around him, who were simple people and prone to panic. The disciples interpreted his command over fear as a command over the situation – and even the elements.

Jesus was calm, not because he was 'on another plane', did not care or was by nature fearless and brave. He was calm because he had 'knowledge' – a belief, intuition and instinct in God's self. These would take care of the boat. These gave him complete command and authority over the situation – and over his own prodigal feelings of fear. "Why are you frightened? Have you no faith?" he retorted. Fear and panic destroys all grace and so God's ability to take care of us.

Jesus did not worry that they had mistaken his commands 'to be still and quiet', which were directed at the pandemonium around him, to be solely directed at the storm. Jesus would have directed those words at a boatful of people either crashing around or sitting paralysed with fear. Both reactions jeopardised the safety of all. Jesus knows what the storm is doing – that such storms vanish as fast as they appear and are short lived. It would look as if he was commanding Nature, rather than announcing the nature of the storm. There is little difference between the two. Knowledge gives us **command and authority**.

There was recently a 'perfect' storm that capsized the Sydney to Hobart yacht race. Twelve boats were sunk and many were drowned. A survivor spoke about his ordeal and fight for survival against all the odds. He said, "There are no rules, nothing out there. No right or wrong. No God. You only have your own instinct, your own idea of what will work or not work". Jesus would have agreed that there was not a God 'out there', in that no hand is going to alter the conditions just for you. He would have also agreed there were no rules ... in such a situation only surviving is what matters. Jesus would have agreed with the man's sentiment about relying on an instinct for what works and does not work. Jesus would have simply taken it all one step further and said, "The instinctive knowledge within you (along with the belief and intuition) is part of the person of God, who is responsible for both you and the storm".

The importance of this lesson in grace lies in its symbolism of our common experience of life. Our lives are 'wavy' – full of ups and downs and sudden storms. We live in a state of 'never really knowing what might happen next'. Jesus offers the experience of grace as a 'stabiliser', which does not modify the storm but our responses to it and so helps keep us on an even keel.

The rich man and the eye of a needle – a lesson in wealth

A rich man came to Jesus to ask what he needed to do in order to enter the Kingdom of Heaven and find its grace. He was a righteous 'good' man who followed all the commandments. Jesus said, "Give all you have to the poor and come and follow me". The rich man was aghast and went away. Jesus told them that 'a rich man had as much chance of getting into the Kingdom as a camel had of passing through the eye of a needle'. The disciples were shocked, saying, "Are we not all doomed then?" They were making the point that everyone strives for prosperity. Nations strive for prosperity and wealth. Money literally makes the world go around. Jesus replies cryptically, "All things are possible with God". Jesus is reiterating here that entering the Kingdom of Heaven has nothing to do with who we are or what we do. We are all prodigal selves – rich, poor, children, old people, saints and sinners. Nothing saves us from our prodigal fate but the Father and His will of generosity. The only thing that can give us grace with that is our own generosity of will – our humility or knowledge of our personal bankruptcy. The rich man is saved not by giving away all his money but realising that his money will not save him (as neither will his moral righteousness).

Jesus tells people not to store up wealth in barns on earth where moths and robbers can destroy it, but store wealth in heaven where it is safe and earns us eternal life. Jesus is not anti–wealth but against not storing up wealth in heaven. Indeed Jesus talks of his followers as 'children of light' who can be slack about money management. He says that people who cannot be trusted to manage something as small as money can hardly be trusted with the 'true riches' of the Kingdom. Good money management and the good use of it, is not the same thing as being mean with it and using it as an alternative to the wealth of the Kingdom. Jesus actually tells his followers, through his **parable of the shrewd manager**, to 'use worldly wealth to gain friends, so that when it has gone, you will be welcomed into heaven'.

Jesus makes strong links in all his stories and teachings between the wealth of heaven and the wealth on earth. The wealth on earth is a consequence of a wealth in heaven and so our use of our wealth on earth must reflect our wealth in heaven. However our wealth on earth cannot buy us wealth in heaven.

What destroys grace or entry to the Kingdom

Jesus identified the root of what makes people stumble, as fear. The prodigal Son lacks a Father to love and be loved by. He feels abandoned and alone and so lives in fear. Jesus repeatedly encourages people, 'do not be afraid!'. It is behind his encouragement to his disciples when he tells them not worry about their life, what they will eat, or what they will wear, but to look at the birds of the field who do not sow or reap, yet God feeds them; and the lilies of the field who do not work or spin, and yet Solomon in all his splendour is not dressed as beautifully. Jesus is not encouraging people to be lazy and is not suggesting the lilies or birds do not "work" – in fact they work very hard to survive. However they do not worry or fear about 'what might happen' like the prodigal Son does. They are faithful and accepting in their lives about what does happen and what is provided for them.

Fear blinds the prodigal or aware Son to his relationship with the Father and the opportunities of grace and what the Father is doing. He becomes occupied with what he thinks is happening or what might happen and does not see what **is** happening.

Fear is what trips us all up. Fear is what made all the disciples stumble as they followed Jesus. It is what made Peter sink in his bid to emulate Jesus' walk on water and deny his fellowship when Jesus needed it most. It made Thomas doubt the spirit of Jesus and it made Judas betray him.

Being sustained by grace

There are a number of 'lesser' miracles or examples where Jesus is seen to find and provide sustenance by grace or noticing opportunities provided by Nature 'or what God is doing'. These little barely noticed 'helping hands' are really what grace is all about, not some blinding supernatural event or 'miracle', that puts grace and our need to partake in it conveniently outside ourselves. Man is saved and sustained by a constant presence of the Trinity within and its grace. This is the truth about grace. It is mundane like the small but vital break given to the victim by the Good Samaritan. Jesus encouraged people not to see events as good or bad 'luck' but as opportunities to do the will of God – to partake in a grace, remain awake and fearless to what 'the Father is doing'.

While Jesus was teaching on the shores of the lake Gennesaret, he saw two boats come ashore. Among the fishermen was Simon Peter who Jesus knew. The fishermen left their boats to wash their nets and Jesus got into one of the boats and asked Simon to push him out so he could hold audience. He told Simon and his friends to go into deeper water and throw their nets. He already knew they had caught no fish all night. Simon obliged and they caught so many fish they filled all the boats. Simon, an experienced fisherman, knew this event was not just a result of Jesus reading the physical signs of the sea, something about which Peter himself was very knowledgeable. This was a result of the intuition of grace with God. Simon fell to his knees before Jesus, as recognition of this and said, "Go away for I am a sinful man". By saying this he inferred that Jesus had grace – a state of forgiveness.

Jesus' spirit does this again after his physical death when in the guise of a 'stranger' he appears on the shore to the disciples. They later recognise this stranger as having the spirit of Jesus in him. He also helps them land a great catch after a fruitless expedition.

Another example of Jesus' grace occurred in Capernaum. Here Jesus was asked for the temple tax. Jesus, as a 'citizen of the country', disapproved of paying taxes to the temple. This was a reference to being a 'citizen of God's country' and citizens did not pay temple taxes in their own country, only foreigners. He was resentful that the Son of Man with the Truth had to pay taxes to the sinful temple, when he had been sent to put things right. He ordered Peter to go to the lake and sling a hook with bait. The first fish he caught would have a coin in its mouth. The denomination would be enough to pay the tax.

The story seems far fetched and bizarre but it cleverly represents that grace is often bizarre. What can be more bizarre than the knowledge of the Trinity itself? There would have been reasons for this coin to have found its way into the fish's mouth. There may have been lots of children throwing coins into the lake at a certain spot – as we all do as kids. There may have been a tradition of throwing coins into this part of the lake. Fish may have been attracted to the 'flashing' reflection of the little coins as they slowly sank, giving an appearance of bait. A fish with a coin stuck in its mouth and gills may, due to its condition, be the hungry fish and the first to bite the hook.

However grace is not a clever conscious way of working all these factors out. It is not an educated guess. It is 'knowledge'. This story is a good representation of the small 'helping hands' that grace gives which together create for us a 'lifetime' of difference.

Grace the healer – "Your faith has healed you"

In Jesus' day medicine, in the modern sense, was completely non-existent. If people became sick then, whether they died or recovered was literally in the 'lap of the Gods'. There may have been rudimentary treatments and remedies which were effective, but many were mumbo jumbo. People had to rely entirely on the body's considerable natural ability to heal itself. Any prophets or 'men of God' were therefore also harbingers of God's mercy and His healing properties. Prophets were always healers and it was no surprise that Jesus' mission began with healing and people flocked to him for healing.

Jesus did not see the healing process as some external magical supernatural power that flowed as mercy from a God above or himself. He saw the healing process as a natural process or state of health that flowed from within a person – something that people allowed to occur within themselves. It was something similar to his teaching of the mustard seed. "If you had as much faith as a mustard seed, you could say to that mountain, 'cast thyself into the sea' and it would be done". The mustard seed allows the tree within it to grow. If we acknowledge that the spiritual wholeness of the Trinity (God's self) lies within us then we acknowledge the physical wholeness of ourselves too or the healing intended for us.

Jesus saw healing as a natural state because he plainly told people that we cannot change the colour of our hair, our height or grow another leg. Health is part of the grace or help of God – a gift – indeed it is in the nature of God. Jesus' grace with God was not something he could give to people but something with which he could inspire people to find the same within themselves. When people found the grace of healing by 'believing in the Jesus' it was really the same as believing in the Trinity within themselves. We see this best in the story of the centurion's servant. The centurion had sought out Jesus to heal a much-loved servant. As is the case with servant hood the servant will have absolute faith in the master. The centurion has complete faith in Jesus' grace with God or power over disease. He tells Jesus so. He says it is the same kind of absolute power he has over his platoon. Jesus remarks that he has not seen such faith. It is therefore of little surprise that Jesus knows that, considering the attitude of the centurion and therefore his relationship with his servant, his servant will already believe that his master has got what he wanted for him – his cure. The servant has complete faith in his master and the master has complete faith in Jesus and Jesus has complete faith in God. In effect the servant had shown complete faith in God within himself. Jesus saw faith and love as the same, both act as inspiration for others to find that which is within them.

There are many other records of Jesus' healing many forms of sickness. In all these instances it is the person's own faith, whoever that faith is expressed through, that results in their healing. Jesus explains this by telling them, "Your faith has healed you".

A person who was blind from birth meets Jesus. Jesus says that this blindness is not due to sin, the person's prodigal nature or his parents. It is not a problem of faith but a natural oddity. He cures him with mud and spittle. Here we see Jesus heal someone with a natural remedy and intuitive knowledge of medicine. This is another important way in which grace helps us to find healing in ourselves – by doing things that are good for our health or naturally promote health.

In another instance Jesus heals a man with a withered arm. Here Jesus frees a person from a psychological paralysis in the same way as he gets the lame to walk. Jesus reveals how the body can return to itself functions when we believe that it can. Psychosomatic diseases would have been particularly prevalent in Jesus' day when ignorance and superstition spawned severe fears and doubts.

A woman who has suffered haemorrhaging for years pushes through the crowds to touch Jesus' cloak, believing if she just touched him she would be cured. She was cured. This again shows the power of healing in the Trinity of self within, the belief it serves us and its profound effect upon the body. Today science is beginning to understand the ability of the mind to impact the physical workings of the body in surprising ways. Hormone levels can be changed, chemical levels altered and it has even been suggested that genes can be switched off or on by our mental state.

Often Jesus talks of healing being achieved by expelling demons. Demons are seen as spirits that occupy the soul. Today we view them as ideas, feelings and actions – doubts or lack of trust, fears, insecurities, lack of self worth, love of power and material wealth. They blind us to reality. Jesus said that if a person's spiritual state can affect and poison the heart, mind and actions then so it can poison their body physically and cause disease. People today believe that their outside habits or lifestyles are paramount in promoting health. Jesus believed that people's habits inside are more important in determining health. He talked about 'the lamp of the body' being the eye, and 'when the eye is good, the whole body also is filled with light. But when your eye is bad, your body also is full of darkness'. He scorned the obsession people had who thought certain foods were unclean, 'for whatever enters the mouth goes into the stomach and is eliminated. But those things which proceed out of the mouth come from the heart, and they defile a man. For out of the heart come evil thoughts, murders, adulteries, thefts, false witness, blasphemies'.

Jesus showed how grace can heal the mentally ill. Again this is not some supernatural magic but the ability of grace to change a person's response to their mental instability – the ability to calm fear and paranoia. This enables a patient to find an equilibrium and space in which to understand and cope with their condition. This is seen as much more effective than modern day drugs. A madman who lives outside the city starts to rant and scream at Jesus. Jesus orders the demons to leave him and the man is becalmed. The demons enter a herd of pigs which are then panicked into running over a cliff.

This story may seem fanciful but is symbolic of the power of grace – the love of the Father in the shared Holy Spirit. The Holy Spirit is not something etherised but a person that inhabits Man and helps the prodigal Son to overcome his prodigal condition with the Father's love. Jesus was keen to demonstrate this. In this story we see the madman recognise the Holy Spirit in Jesus and therefore accept its presence in himself. The change from frothing madness to serenity that occurs in this man on finding the help of the Holy Spirit within, startles the pigs and it was this that made them stampede over the cliff. The demons in the shape of their own fear drive the pigs to self destruction, just as they were driving the madman to self destruction.

Jesus makes a further reference to this concept of demons occupying the soul in a comment he makes about keeping our 'house' clean. He refers to the dawn of grace (being born again) as a process of the soul or 'our house' being swept clean of demons (prodigal thoughts, feelings and actions or habits). He warns that this house must be then filled with the Father, Son and Holy Spirit, for if it is left vacant, then the demons will tell their friends and come back to the house and it will be worse off than before.

In another case Jesus meets a man's son, after the disciples have been unable to heal him. The man asks Jesus if he can heal him. The man has already admitted that he does not have complete faith. The boy has had fits from birth and is uncommunicative, a condition that is very influenced by the person's (and those close to them) emotional and spiritual health. Jesus replies, "Yes, if you yourself can". Again Jesus refers to the necessity of the sufferer or their guardian to have complete faith in their own self's capacity to heal. Jesus says, "Everything is possible for him who has faith". The father makes the correct reply saying, "I do have faith, but not enough. Help me have more." The man, by saying this, recognises complete faith (in Jesus) because he knows he does not have it. Here we see the example of Jesus' complete faith inspire another person to recognise it and entertain it as a possibility within himself. Only now does Jesus decide that the 'demon' in the boy can be driven out.

Jesus tells the disciples that only prayer can heal the boy's illness. By this he means that, because the father's faith is incomplete, Jesus must 'connect' with the child directly through the common Trinity or self of God that all people share. He speaks to and inspires the child not through the father's faith but directly by the common self of God. Jesus alludes to the fact that all humans are connected spiritually and physically (in mind, heart and body) as one. Therefore the faith of one can become the faith of another, if we connect (i.e. give and receive) – even over space and time. That can be possible because it is a spiritual connection. People can be in harmony like a huge flock of birds that fly together with a collective intuition and grace – as one heart, mind and body.

The raising of Lazarus – grace in the unconscious

Jesus was across the River Jordan, visiting where John the Baptist preached. He was told that Lazarus was ill. Jesus was a good friend of the family, Martha, her sister Mary and their brother Lazarus. Jesus said that the illness would not be fatal. Jesus knew by the knowledge of grace what would happen – what God was doing. He said, "This has happened in order to glorify God and people will be amazed by the Son of God". He is saying that this event is an opportunity for him to show people how God works and expresses himself. He deliberately waited two days then decided to go to Lazarus' home. He made no attempt to heal Lazarus because he knew that Lazarus would slip into a coma or death like state. This is not uncommon and there have been well documented cases, even today with our advanced medical technology, of people in a catatonic state being pronounced dead only to regain consciousness in the mortuary. It is not common however to know, from a distance, that someone is suffering this state.

The disciples tried to stop Jesus from going, for he was hated in Judea and they had already tried to kill him there. Again he makes a reference to his short life, saying "that they were living in the day, but night would follow day when the light would not be there. So he must work!" He says that Lazarus is asleep and he will wake him. The disciples say that if he is asleep, he will get better, so why bother to go! Jesus cannot explain the 'state of unconsciousness' that Lazarus is in, other than he 'sleeps'. People had little understanding of the states of unconsciousness. So to avoid argument as to whether they should go or not, Jesus says, "O.K. He is dead and for your sake I am glad I was not there and you will believe". He is saying 'if you want to call him dead then you will make this awakening even more of a miracle'. Jesus ends the argument and says, "Let's go to him". Thomas mutters, "Let's all go with the Teacher, so that we may die (get killed) with him!"

When they arrive Lazarus has been 'dead and buried' for four days. Both Martha and Mary almost tell Jesus off for not coming sooner and healing Lazarus. Jesus says to Martha, "I am the resurrection and the Life. Those that believe in me will live even though they die, and all those who live and believe in me will never die. Do you believe this?" It is here that Jesus is making sure they understand the true spiritual significance of the term 'to not die'. It does not mean evading a physical death, from which there is no escape. Death is part of 'what God is doing' or the natural preordination of creation. He knows that, like everyone else, they believe that Lazarus is dead and nothing he can do will convince them otherwise. Jesus does not want to force them into believing otherwise. He knows they will believe that he has brought Lazarus back from the dead (which is not in the will of God or a part of grace), so he wants to use this 'miracle' to teach them about the real nature of eternal life. He wants to demonstrate that it is grace that will raise Lazarus from the unconscious, just as it is grace that can resurrect us after we have died – both spiritually and physically.

They will see Lazarus raised from the 'death of unconsciousness' just as we are raised or resurrected after our death of the physical.

Because everyone assumed Lazarus was dead, a full mourning was in progress and Jesus was now moved by their grief. He was not moved by his own grief but touched by their affection for Lazarus. This is empathy. He ends up in tears himself. Everyone said, "See how he loved Lazarus". However why should Jesus mourn for he knows Lazarus is not dead – but 'sleeps'. He asks them to lead him to the tomb and roll the stone away. Martha warns him about the smell from his rotting body. They take the stone away and there is no smell. Lazarus is not dead. Jesus knows that there will be no smell but he is relieved! He gives thanks to God for 'listening to him'. This is a clear reference to Jesus communing with God over the nature of Lazarus' illness and God has given him the correct information – by intuition. He goes on to say, "I know that you always listen to me (a reference to himself being in grace with God and God tells him everything) but I say this for the sake of the people here, so that they believe that you sent me".

Jesus is having this conversation with God out aloud, so that people understand that his abilities are not some personal supernatural power, but a consequence of a grace or relationship with

God. He says this here because he knows these people believe Lazarus is dead and so will be amazed by his 'awakening'. Jesus is therefore taking special advantage of this 'miracle' to get the message of grace across and it is not magic. He then says 'in a loud voice' so Lazarus could hear in his unconscious state, "Lazarus. Come out!" It is often the case that people arise suddenly from a comatose state in response to a powerful emotion of love associated with sounds – familiar music, people's voices etc. People who have arisen from comas tell of being devoid of all senses except the sense of hearing. Jesus carried enormous charisma for those who understood who he was, as Lazarus did. Lazarus was an ardent supporter and follower of Jesus and had had attempts made on his life because of this. Jesus' voice would have engendered such love and excitement in Lazarus as to be the stimulus needed to awaken him.

Lazarus emerged from his tomb, bound hand and foot with a cloth over his face. This meant that he came immediately to consciousness and struggled to the tomb entrance. Tombs were in those days no more than a small hole in the rock and Lazarus would have struggled out into the daylight. Jesus here proves that the profound unconsciousness of a coma is no barrier to grace, as neither will our physical death be at the end of our lives.

Chapter Seven

The Prodigal Disciples

Grace gives Man a knowledge of people and their nature. While Jesus was in Jerusalem during the Passover, many believed in him as they saw the miracles he performed. It was said, "But Jesus did not trust himself to them, because he knew them all. There was no need for any one to tell him about them, because he himself knew what was in their hearts". Grace gives the power of insight into people or 'what they are doing' – just as God's self does. In this case Jesus could not trust them, as they believed what he did but did not understand how he did these things and so 'who' he was.

On another occasion Jesus knew immediately, on meeting a Samaritan woman by a well, everything about her. He proceeded to tell her everything about her life so that she was convinced of Jesus' power and listened to him and what he had to say about God's self within Man and was converted.

There are numerous instances where Jesus amazed people with his ability to predict what people were going to do and say. Much of his insight stemmed from his knowledge of a person's prodigal self. He knew well the behaviour of the three types. When a prodigal body (Brute), the rich and pious man (both materially and morally wealthy!), comes to him and asks what he needs to do to enter the Kingdom, Jesus tells him to give away all his material possessions. The man retreats disappointed. Jesus has gone straight to the prodigal body and challenged it as to how keen it was for redemption. When a prodigal heart (Lucifer) comes to Jesus and asks if he can follow him, Jesus goes straight for the prodigal heart to find out how keen he is on redemption. Jesus tells him to come, but the man says he first wants to bury his father. Jesus says he wants no-one in his following who is constantly looking behind for the 'loves' they left behind; 'let the dead bury the dead'. When a prodigal mind comes to him (the snake), a lawyer named Nicodemus, he wants Jesus to explain how 'a man can be born again'. He cannot understand with his prodigal mind the secret of the Trinity within. Jesus stays all night while Nicodemus challenges Jesus with his prodigal mind. Nicodemus is 'blinded' by his prodigal mind.

Contrast this with his meeting with a prodigal mind that does 'see'. Zacchaus listens earnestly to Jesus' teaching, and being a short man and wanting to see Jesus, he climbs a tree. Jesus spots him and invites him over to be with him. Jesus gets himself invited back to Zacchaus' home. Zacchaus sees the Truth, the Life and the Way and is converted. He symbolically gives up the prodigal mind by accepting the Truth into himself and says he will give away half his wealth, all that he has stolen and tricked from people (the prodigal half body). Prodigal minds build wealth largely not through hard and honest graft (as prodigal bodies do) but by cleverness and trickery.

Jesus would have deduced Hitler as being a prodigal mind by his famous comment about religion. "Religion is a joint stock company set up for the exploitation of the stupid". His fully prodigal mind scoffs at the 'stupid' idea of a Father. He describes his own spiritual emptiness in the heart and half body by calling it a joint stock company! He is describing the view of the snake form of Satan, who always become the charismatic 'hearts', and so leaders of satanic cults.

Jesus knew the prodigal selves of his disciples. He knew therefore where their weaknesses lay and predicted their actions. He understood Judas' lack of trust (prodigal body) and predicted his betrayal and remorse. He understood Peter's lack of faith (prodigal heart) and predicted his denial and remorse.

He understood Thomas' lack of belief (prodigal mind) and helped him with his doubting by asking him to feel his wounds.

Jesus deliberately chose the three prodigal types in his twelve disciples, four of each. Furthermore he chose disciples who were strongly prodigal in nature. He knew such people were weary of their prodigal selves and disillusioned with their prodigal fathers – so were keen to find the freedom of the Kingdom of Heaven – and God's help. They were hungry for redemption. They were, with Jesus' help, going to find redemption from a place they least expected – from within themselves.

Furthermore Jesus knew strong enemies (prodigal selves) make, when won over, the strongest allies. These disciples needed to have both great hunger and qualities of endurance, conviction and strength. They were going to be chosen to lay the foundations of a new philosophy, self awareness and the Kingdom on earth after Jesus had gone. They had to be able to carry his torch. They were to be the 'new skins' into which Jesus would pour 'new wine'. New wine is the euphemism that Jesus used to describe his new Truth or philosophy.

Peter was the archetype of the prodigal heart or Lucifer – garrulous, emotional, unsteady and tempestuous as well as warm hearted, gregarious and generous. He was Jesus' natural choice to build his church upon. Jesus called him his 'rock', giving him his new name (Cephus) Peter which means 'rock'. He declared almost immediately that Peter would be in charge of his church or fellowship in earth. The fellowship or body is in the Father's half of Lucifer and Jesus aimed to show Peter that half of himself – the body/fellowship of the Father. Jesus would show Peter that the Father's self was as much a part of himself as his prodigal self.

Peter had a trusting acceptance of Jesus. Peter sees God's self (the Trinity) in Jesus on the meeting on the shore, after Jesus helps Peter's boat crew find a fish shoal. He falls to his knees and tells Jesus to go away and calls Jesus, 'a man without sin'. This is the moment when Peter finds the Father within him – the fellowship and half mind of the Father. He sees the Way and half the Truth. He therefore acknowledges the prodigal half of himself and its need for redemption by the Father. He sees his prodigal self as a construct of Original Sin and shows his humility, calling himself 'unworthy' of Jesus. However Jesus affirms he is worthy of the Father, asks Peter to follow him and soon renames him Cephus or 'rock'. Peter is not unworthy, but will be Jesus' 'rock'.

However Peter has not found the place of the prodigal Son in the Holy Spirit, its acceptance by the Father. He is not born again in the Holy Spirit and does not receive the help of the Holy Spirit. So we see Peter's prodigal self helplessly let Jesus (the Father within) down again and again. Jesus is patient, constantly sweeping up after Peter and helping when he stumbles. We see Peter's prodigal self (prodigal heart and half mind) when he tries to follow Jesus to walk on water. He shows great fellowship and bodily enthusiasm (trust in the Father) and some belief (half belief in the Father), when he steps out onto the water. It carries him some distance before his prodigal heart (lack of faith) and half mind (shaky belief) lets him down and he sinks. Again his prodigal heart or lack of faith fails him when he denies Jesus three times after Jesus' arrest. After professing his prodigal love boldly and repeatedly for Jesus, he predictably fails the test of true love (faith) when Jesus needed him most in the fellowship. Peter lets Jesus down when he attacks one of the people come to arrest Jesus in the garden. Peter's prodigal heart with its passion rules over any trust again. Jesus has to smooth over the waters kicked up by Peter, this time by healing the man's ear which Peter almost hacked off. The ear is made up of cartilage and the flesh covering has a good blood supply. If bound in place immediately it will heal quickly. As much as anything the soldier and the arresting officers would have been surprised by the act of Jesus showing so much concern for his enemy – an important symbol of healing on a spiritual level too.

Only after Jesus' death does Peter reaffirm (three times) his love for Jesus to the 'stranger' on the shore, who cooks the disciples a fish barbecue. When people in Jesus' day professed something three times it was binding for eternity. This time Peter is 'born again' and the Father and prodigal Son within him are bound together by their common will and love in the person of the Holy Spirit. Peter now has belief, faith and trust in the Holy Spirit.

Judas was the archetype of the prodigal body or Brute. Jesus seeks him out as a confidante and personal assistant to himself and the disciples, in charge of their physical welfare. Jesus is close to Judas and trusts him with the disciples' affairs and money. Jesus knows this is his prodigal strength – the body. However this is also the disciple who best understands the Truth or mind of Jesus. In Jesus he sees and finds the Father within him (the mind and half heart of the Father). He therefore acknowledges the prodigal self and its need for redemption. In the debated 'Gospel of Judas' it is Judas who declares he sees the Truth in Jesus and lowers his eyes in humility. It is he who is pulled aside by Jesus to be instructed in the 'secrets of the Kingdom of Heaven'. In Jesus' eyes Judas is the only one worthy of the secret. To the others Jesus says the Truth is 'too much to bear and the Holy Spirit will lead Mankind into all the Truth – eventually'. The whole Truth is that the persons of the Father, Son and Holy Spirit or God's self lie within all people. In this gospel Jesus gives Judas comfort, as he does to Peter, concerning his future failings, by predicting them and forgiving them in his own absence. He shows him a star in the sky, a cold distant speck of light, and tells him that it is his guiding star and it will lead him home. He suggests that Judas will enter a dark place and it is his strength in belief alone that will pull him through – his appreciation of the Truth. He tells Judas that he will be spurned by a generation (everyone) but will one day rule over all generations (everyone). This is a reference to the Truth being a late flowerer in the story of the Trinity – "The whole Truth is too much for you to bear now". This a moving story as it shows Jesus helping the prodigal self of Judas to redemption. Of all the disciples his future is the blackest and bleakest and the image of a speck of light (hope) that Jesus places in the sky for him will make all the difference to Judas when he is on his own with his remorse.

Judas' prodigal self lets Jesus down in a most famous and spectacular way – the betrayal. However there are the odd inferences in the gospels to Judas being miserly with money. He complains about the waste of money when Jesus' feet are anointed with a very expensive bottle of oil by Mary, saying the money would have been better spent on the poor who needed it most. He does not share Peter's and the others' feelings that Jesus is 'worth' it. Judas shows all the traits of prodigal bodies who do not like inefficiency or waste. His parsimony is resented and typically rumours and suspicions circulate that he is thieving money form the coffers.

Judas, by mutual agreement with Jesus, brokers a deal (ever the businessman) with the authorities, Jesus' enemies, for Jesus to be taken unharmed. It is Judas' job after all to look after everyone physically. After Jesus' attack on the Temple traders, the religious authorities stepped up their attempts to have Jesus killed. Jesus goes along with Judas' plan to lead the authorities to Jesus in return for him not to be harmed and a deal negotiated. Judas cannot see that Jesus' Truth is a very profound threat to the authorities. Jesus, however, can see this and knows his fate already. He knows Judas' plan will go horribly wrong. Judas also does not understand, as the prodigal body, why Jesus has to die and make a willing sacrifice of his body in order for the Truth to be revealed in people. Judas has not been born again in the Holy Spirit and cannot comprehend the Way.

Poor Judas, as Jesus predicted, incurs the wrath of everybody when the plan goes horribly wrong (but spiritually right!) and Jesus is subjected to a ghastly, humiliating death in the space of few swift, brutal hours. Jesus warns Judas that 'for the betrayer it is better that he was not born at all'. He will be reviled by all and be filled with a terrible self reproach. It proved correct. Judas realises how his position is now untenable, and there is no way out for him but to commit suicide. However Judas is very remorseful and throws away the blood money (a customary payment for such an act) that the Pharisees gave him – and hangs himself. Judas is 'born again' as he accepts the fate given to him and shows a humble remorse, as Peter did. He realises the loving Father and humble prodigal Son in the person of the Holy Spirit.

Thomas is the archetype of the prodigal mind or snake (the prodigal mind and half body). He accepts and sees his Father's half in Jesus' heart. In doing so he acknowledges his prodigal self or half and its need for redemption. He is very faithful and loyal to Jesus throughout his ministry but does not see the Truth. He stumbles along in a 'blind' faith. When Jesus dies his faith is 'lost' and he crumbles. He lacks belief, and his prodigal mind and half body lets him down spectacularly before the spiritual body or apparition of Jesus, when he appears before the disciples. He refuses to believe that the apparition is real and our language carries the expression 'doubting Thomas' to this day. Thomas believed in the Father and accepted the prodigal Son but was not 'born again in the Spirit'. He did not share the same will or love with the Father in the person of the Holy Spirit.

Jesus tells Thomas to place his fingers in the wound in his side. He encourages Thomas to abandon his prodigal mind and half body and believe and complete his trust. Thomas obeys this and the Father and prodigal Son within him are made one in the person of the Holy Spirit. Thomas believes and so his belief serves him with its reality and he can 'feel' Jesus' body to be real, just as the guests in Cana tasted wine.

Each disciple goes on a journey of self discovery – the discovery of the three persons of God's self within them. They are shown the Father within them and the prodigal Son. Jesus then leads each disciple by his own example to the 'narrow gate' or humility of the prodigal Son and his need for redemption. In this humility of the prodigal Son the disciples each recognise their (as prodigal Sons) own part or will in the person of the Holy Spirit. They recognise their shared will with the Father in this person – and so the redemption of the prodigal Son. In this person of the Holy Spirit the humble prodigal Son is redeemed by the Father's love and forgiveness and acceptance of the prodigal Son, exactly as he is. But it is a hard road for all, not least for Jesus. He shows his frustration with their prodigal selves when he cries, "Oh how long do I have to put up with you all!" But in the end at the last supper he thanks God that he has not lost any of the disciples (except Judas, as the spiritual story required) and prays not for the world but the disciples.

Chapter Eight

The Christian Story

Jesus the boy

Jesus was the man, the prodigal self, who was destined to lead a prodigal world to grace, salvation or the Kingdom of Heaven. He was to make man aware of the true nature of self and so Life – that self is a Trinity. Jesus' early life possessed a number of unusual psychological or spiritual characteristics and experiences that predisposed him to that destiny.

Jesus' life, as any person's life, cannot be studied in isolation. His coming was prophesised and his destiny supported by many – not least his disciples. Prophesy is not something that is otherworldly or supernatural, but very much a product of this world. It has a function of identifying and focusing people on a goal – the fulfilment of a need. It was prophesised that a Messiah would come three hundred years before Jesus; a man who would bring not religious laws but grace. People were crying out for grace, for religious laws were getting people nowhere. People were desperate for liberation not just from the Romans but from religious laws and their hypocrisy. Jesus told his disciples that the 'harvest was white' – people desired the Truth.

Prophesies would be made and woven into stories and handed down into the generations, so all people were aware of them and could collectively conspire to fulfil them. It was prophesised that a leader would come from Bethlehem in Judah, who would guide the people of Israel, the Jews. Also in those days natural events, particularly in the mysterious heaven, such as the appearance of a comet, bright star or the lining up of planets would be interpreted as signs from God, and so add credence to a prophesy. When a bright star appeared in the sky in 4 B.C. it would have galvanised astrologers, astronomers, wise men or magi into making their assessments and interpretations. Prophesy has the function of bringing people and events together into a 'conspiracy to make true'. The conspiracy in this case was focusing on the person of Jesus. Such a star would have heralded a great event and there was none greater than the forecast of the coming of the King of the Jews or Messiah. Tensions in Palestine were boiling and there had been periodically revolutionaries and brigands who claimed to be the Messiah, but all proved to be false. People were desperate for someone with authority who could rid the Jews of the Romans.

When wise men arrived in Jerusalem with their news of the coming of the Messiah, King Herod the puppet king of the Romans would have been upset, as apparently everyone else in the city was too. People would have held great store by what the religious priests and lawyers, astrologers and philosophers said. Kings would have consulted them and acted on their advice. The whole city would be aware of their news. When Herod asked the men where the child would be born, the priests quoted the scriptures and told him it would be Bethlehem. So it was no surprise when they followed the star it stopped where they stopped – Bethlehem! The presence of oxen at the birth would not have been unusual in a humble home of the times. Stables were combined within homes and the cattle used to keep the occupants warm. It would not even have been unusual to see oxen kneel when they become interested in something like a crib near the ground. It is natural and harmless that people see signs wherever they can, when they wish for some belief to be confirmed. These signs have a scientific basis, but this does not mean they are mindless or random and without spiritual meaning, significance and consequences. Jesus himself would say that it is belief that makes sense of what we see rather than the other way around.

At the time of Jesus, life was desperate and dangerous. People lived in perpetual fear of death, disease, disaster, famine and violence. Herod had already made a bid to get rid of this Messiah, by ordering a mass slaughter of all babies in the land, a cruelty that defies belief today. People would have been at their wits' end and they would have tended to hand over decision making to the unconscious or God. This might mean being given guidance through dreams. God was seen to speak to people through the unconscious – as in dreams. The unconscious is really the core of Man's mind, the common self; that part of us still in touch with or in grace with God's self. So Joseph is instructed by God in dreams to escape from Herod and then when the time is right to return from exile to Galilee. It is not fanciful to say that God protected and guided Joseph through his intuition, because he believed and trusted in his unconscious and all that flowed from it. Being in grace or touch with God's self means having access to all that is in the universe, all that God has. It is at the heart of religious belief and faith and Joseph was a religious man – 'a man who always did that which was right'.

The virgin birth was prophesised. "A virgin will become pregnant and have a son; and he will be called Emmanuel (which means God is with us)'. Prophets decide what should happen and then it is engineered to happen, as described in Matthew. "Now all this happened in order to make what the Lord had said through the prophet come true". This man was to be God incarnate, the Son of God or a man who possessed God's self. People could not conceive of this happening in an ordinary man. Although there was no knowledge of genetics they knew a person inherited their father and mother's traits. It was an easy and perfectly logical step to have the Holy Spirit or spirit of God the Father being the Father. People had no concept of the biology of sexual reproduction and they had no science to tell them that such a thing was impossible.

In fact Mary gets pregnant before they are married and an angel tells Mary that she is going to give birth to a saviour, after being made pregnant by God the Holy Spirit. Genealogy was very important in these tribal people. Jesus, as well as being the Son of God, was also a direct descendent of the royal house of David through Joseph. Only Mary knew the truth. Joseph was made aware that Mary was pregnant while they were engaged. Joseph was keen to protect Mary from public disgrace. In these times it would have been a catastrophe to become pregnant out of wedlock – for whatever reason. It would have meant a ruination and disgrace (even death) for Mary and her family impossible to understand in a 'post war' liberal society. Single mothers were outcasts and treated no better than prostitutes. Joseph was a man who 'always did that which was right'. He set out to withdraw privately to spare Mary the public disgrace. He would not of course marry a woman who was to bear another man's son. However Joseph had a dream in which an angel told him to marry Mary – to make an 'honest woman' of her. So he did. Both Joseph and Mary now believe that this child is to be the Son of God and saviour of Mankind. Both parents would have made it clear to friends and neighbours that Jesus was the saviour. The news would have travelled widely. Communities, even important cities, would have had an intimacy that is not imaginable today. People did not travel as much or so quickly and would have been more closely related (hence the importance of knowing your genealogy!). So news would have travelled widely by a grapevine of intimate gossip. Officials in Jerusalem may have heard about Jesus and then mentioned it to the wise men. By their visit to the manger, the wise men went on to 'confirm' Jesus' birthright to the inhabitants of Bethlehem, to Mary, Joseph and Jesus and by so doing, confirmed it in themselves. The bright star, of which there is astronomical evidence of its existence, would have been in the same direction as Bethlehem and the star would have stopped when they stopped in Bethlehem and appeared to shine upon Bethlehem. They had no understanding of what stars were.

The prophecy was also confirmed by Elizabeth, the mother of John the Baptist and Mary's cousin. Then again the shepherds confirmed his birth with a visit. They would already have had a local knowledge of this prophecy about Jesus. Then Simeon confirms Jesus' greatness when Joseph and Mary take Jesus to the Temple in Jerusalem for purification. Then an old prophet, a widow named Anna, who never left the Temple, also confirms Jesus as the child who was to set Jerusalem free. There would have been a great urge among people to affirm the prophecy and people would have felt they had received signs to do so, just like the visitations of 'angels' to the shepherds. These signs interpreted as 'angels' would have been merely unusual natural occurrences such as unfamiliar lights in the sky, cloud formations or sounds. These were people with no scientific education at all. A man who captured the imagination of such people was a danger to the authority of their rulers. To such people a relationship with God or 'covenant' was immensely important. Messiahs were bearers of covenants and so also bearers of social justice and new political structures. These covenants, once they captured the imagination of people, had the potential to become social, legal and political movements which could liberate them from real oppression and poverty as well as from their own fears and anxieties. The Messiah was a social phenomenon which has no equivalent in our psyche today.

John says in Chapter 1 of his gospel that people who believed in Christ (the anointed one) were 'given the right to become God's children. They did not become God's children by natural means, by being born again as the children of a human father; but God Himself became their father'. Here John himself talks of how a Christian becomes a child of God, no longer governed by his father's genes, wishes, behaviour, beliefs, standing or love but by God the Father's. He described how there was a world of difference between prodigal love and God's love. Jesus' parents both disowned him as a son of their own prodigal selves and declared him as a Son of God. Jesus was therefore 'untainted' by his parent's prodigal love, all its pressures and all its vagaries.

Yet Jesus had an unremarkable childhood with his brothers who were born after him. His parents were devout and middle class, his father being a craftsman. Jesus would have done the chores, gone to school and played. He would have been much loved, as were all his siblings, but he would have received something different to the others, which would have been critical in shaping him for his role as a saviour.

Jesus was an illegitimate son, possibly the result of a forced union with a Roman soldier (as related by the Jews), which would not have been uncommon. For a pious woman like Mary it would have been a deeply distressing experience full of bitterness, self reproach and disgust. When she found she was pregnant she would have been beside herself and filled with feelings of revulsion for the child. When Joseph found out he would have battled with feelings of anger, hurt pride and rejection of Mary on account of her defilement. If they were to marry and bring up the child as their own, as their consciences dictated, both would have had to dig deep within themselves to find a love that can truly overcome such natural human feelings. They would need such a love to love each other with. With such an illegitimate baby, the healing outcome of Joseph and Mary holding their heads up high, marrying and going on to produce a family without a trace of bitterness and resentment would have been nothing short of miraculous in those days. It is unsurprising that they should find God in their soul searching (and God find them) in the realm of their dreams.

The love Jesus' parents found was a love that came from meeting the Holy Spirit, being born again in the spirit. It arose from their own humility or decision to offer their humility to God. In doing so they found the person of the Holy Spirit within them, its help and the love and wealth of the Father. They received the help of the Spirit to overcome their prodigal selves and love Jesus with the love of the Father. This would have given Jesus a unique upbringing and unique relationship with his parents. Even adoptive or foster parents do not love with this kind of love as they simply become surrogate prodigal parents exercising familial love. Joseph and Mary however rejected familial or prodigal love (their ownership of Jesus as their son) for Jesus and brought up Jesus as if he were God's son only. It is the only way they could cope with their trauma and still raise Jesus with all the love they knew he deserved.

This would have had a huge impact on the child Jesus, particularly if this approach was supported and affirmed by everyone else around and within the family. Even if it was not physically a virgin birth, it would have been psychologically a 'virgin' birth. When we, as prodigal Sons, ourselves are 'born again in the Spirit' and our wills are united with the Father's will in the person of the Holy Spirit this is in effect a 'virgin birth' or the physical prodigal Son being born without a prodigal father. People feel born again with a new non-physical Father. As Jesus later says himself, what we experience as 'knowledge' in ourselves serves us with our belief which serves us with that belief's reality. Jesus would have believed he was a 'Son of God' and experienced it (as God's love) from his parents and those around him and so would have seen the reality of his belief come true.

We can see records of the fruits of this upbringing very early on in Jesus' life. He was allowed a freedom from the constrictions of familial love – a freedom of mind, heart and fellowship. Stories tell of his precocious maturity and freedom of thought. At twelve years old he is misplaced by his parents in Jerusalem during the Passover. His parents travel back in the direction of home for a day without him before noticing that he is missing. This, in its self, shows they afforded him an almost adult lack of supervision. Only three days later do they find him in the Temple conversing like an adult with Jewish teachers. Everyone is amazed at his understanding of the scriptures. Jesus is behaving like a child prodigy. He has shown an enormous resourcefulness and independence in mind, heart and fellowship in fending for himself for three days. He also chides his mother for being worried and for not realising that he would be in his Father's house. He was reminding his mother who he was – the

Son of God. He did not view his parents like others would, as others would expect their parents to worry. It is recorded though that Mary 'treasured these things (incidents) in her heart'. She delighted in them as fruits of God's love. This means they were not isolated incidents but a pattern of behaviour and they did not grate with her maternal instincts. Yet Jesus selflessly honoured his parents and 'obeyed his parents in his childhood'.

Later Jesus returns to this rejection of familial love when he is on his mission. People tell him that his family are outside and want to see him. He says, looking at the people sitting in a circle around him, "Here are my mother and my brothers; whoever does God's will is my mother and brother and sister". Jesus rejects the family, tribe and nation for a fellowship of the Holy Spirit in Mankind. At the wedding of Cana, he again reveals the nature of his relationship with his mother. His mother tells him the wine has run out, almost demanding that he do something. He rebukes her saying, "Do not tell me what to do. My time has yet not come". He is telling her that his time is now his own until his death. He serves his Father's will in the Holy Spirit foremost. She must relinquish him. Mary responds quietly to the others, "Do whatever he tells you". We see the mother bow to the authority of the son, which would have been unusual in a Jewish family, where obeying your parents would have been a life long commitment.

On the cross, as Jesus is dying, he commands Andrew to be a son to his mother and his mother to be Andrew's mother. He views familial love to be a love that can exist between any two human beings, not just blood relatives. Again this would have been an unusual gesture in his culture, where lineage dictated your relationships. Earlier he tells his disciples that people who love their family more than him (God's self) had better go home now. They cannot enter the Kingdom of Heaven. He finally issues a dark warning about the consequences of giving in to this prodigal love by saying, "Your worst enemy is in your own household". He is warning that the kind of love that people have for their own family is unhealthy, harmful for them and for the people they love.

Jesus the Messiah

John the Baptist was a wild, maverick preacher who baptised people in the River Jordan. He was educated in the scriptures and quoted them when asked about his identity. He said he was "the voice of someone shouting in the desert; make a straight path for the Lord to travel". Here again we see a fulfilment of the scriptures. The people were like a desert; people were thirsty and lost and he shouted for them. The Messiah would need someone to introduce him to this parched and desperate world. John would form a sort of stepping stone for that person to enter it. He was both pointing the people towards the Messiah and the Messiah towards the people. John was almost the personification of the people's need for a Messiah – a loud, urgent, almost desperate (to the point of craziness) and wild man, who dressed in skins and lived in a cave.

John and Jesus would not have been entirely strangers, being related. John was a sort of trigger for Jesus' mission. Jesus may have felt many things about himself; even a sense of destiny, but did not know where, when and how he would get there. There was a growing mood of rebellion and despair on more than one level. People wanted to be free of the Romans, the hypocritical and corrupt Pharisees, restrictive religious practice and from their own prodigal prisons. John could see the time was ripe and tells Jesus it is. Jesus tells his disciples the time is ripe, the world is ready for him – "The harvest is white".

Jesus meets the call of Mankind when John baptises him. Jesus was attracted to the increasing commotion that John was creating on the banks of the River Jordan. He affirms who Jesus is by calling him the 'Lamb of God'. This is a reference to Jesus as a prodigal mind – his heart being the heart of God the Father. John is a loud noisy prodigal body but with the mind of God the Father. His vision or mind sets a fire in Jesus' heart who then hands the torch onto Peter's fellowship. John has told people of Jesus who will not baptise people with water but with fire (the love of the person of Holy Spirit). John tells Jesus that it should be him being baptised by Jesus, but Jesus insists that John baptises him. He shows his humility as a prodigal Son and needs John's blessing and affirmation. This ritual is being performed outside the authority of the Jewish church. When Jesus is baptised 'John sees the Holy Spirit descend like a dove'. What John is describing here, in the suitable imagery of the time, is Jesus undergoing a change. This is the moment when John witnesses Jesus 'being born again' or realises the person of the Holy Spirit and so the Father and Son. God's self only comes alive within someone when it is recognised by that person. Now John hears a voice saying, "This is my dear son with whom I am well pleased". This 'inner voice' is a reflection of John's own belief or conviction that Jesus is the 'anointed one' or Christ – the Messiah. This voice also reflects what is occurring within Jesus. He experiences the love and forgiveness of the Father in the person of the Holy Spirit. The Father accepts the prodigal Son as he is – bankrupt. He is well pleased with the prodigal Son simply because he returns.

John has recognised the special destiny in Jesus, the qualifications of his special upbringing and his parents' special love (of the Holy Spirit). In so doing he has brought all this to life and awareness in Jesus. However, as it is written in John's gospel, Jesus still seems unsure. Jesus revisits John the next day and walks past as if to get a response. John responds emphatically again! "There goes the Lamb of God", he yells. Two of John's disciples follow Jesus and he turns and asks them what they want. They say they want Jesus to take them to where he is staying. Jesus took them back with him and they talked for the rest of the day. One of them was Andrew, Simon Peter's brother. After they had talked to Jesus, they were convinced that they had found the Messiah. They went and told Simon Peter who went to see Jesus. It is as if Jesus is at this point testing the water, testing his ideas on some trusted people.

After 'being born again in the Spirit' and discovering God's self within, Jesus went into the wilderness to be alone. He had to fully understand the nature of God's self as the Trinity of persons. The answer was grace. The humility of the prodigal or aware Son (or knowledge of his own bankruptcy) is what opens the door to the Father by the person of the Helper or Holy Spirit. Satan, as the arrogant prodigal self, tests Jesus' apparent lack of power as Son of God or a person with God's self. Jesus realises that his power lies in the grace or help of the Holy Spirit.

Jesus draws up a new covenant – one of grace. It was not the liberation people expected. In fact most people scoffed at the idea he was the Messiah. He was rejected by his own siblings and by Nazareth, his own home town. He entered the synagogue there and inferred he was the Messiah and news of him had already spread there. Prophets led people out of exile, healed diseases, brought relief to the poor and set the oppressed free. Though they marvelled at his eloquence, they could not see this meek and humble man as the Messiah. Was he not the carpenter's son? Precocious he may have been as a child but the Son of God? It was the same reaction as anyone would give if their close friend declared he was the Son of God. There may have been rumours about him before he had arrived back in Nazareth. Jesus said they would receive nothing from him for prophets are never received or welcome in their own home, as Elisha and Elijah were not welcome in Israel. Jesus shows insight into where his new covenant will be sowed. The people in the synagogue were furious and attacked him and tried to throw him off a cliff. This incident shows the risk Jesus was taking by speaking out in such a barbaric, dangerous and lawless society. The priests had real and visible power. It was the law of the Pharisees that 'no-one could testify on their own behalf'. No-one could say that they had God within them or that they were God. Jesus said to them, "Yes, I do testify on my behalf. What I say is true. I know where I come from and where I am going to". To the Pharisees this carried the death sentence and Jesus knew it. His fate was sealed.

Jesus was not insulting Nazareth but was warning them that believing in him and the God within him would lead them to the

God inside themselves. This would set them free. If they ridiculed or rejected him they only rejected and ridiculed the God within themselves. People could not believe that Jesus could talk without an education in such matters. They said, "How can a man say these things without training?" They could not conceive of a knowledge coming solely from within a person – and not as the product of culture and education. Jesus had come from 'nowhere'.

Jesus antagonised the authorities with his empowerment of the individual – that God's self or 'Kingdom' dwelt within all people as the persons of the Father, Son and Holy Spirit. He said that the prodigal Son (each of us) could be redeemed and so share in the Father's Kingdom, by virtue of his own humility alone. At the end of time the prodigal Son can be resurrected in the Kingdom to eternal life, not by great works or morality but by his own humility alone – the knowledge of his own bankruptcy. The Kingdom or person that they saw in him was shared by all people and had an eternal life. After his death people would see this Kingdom still 'alive' in people and themselves. At the end of time this Kingdom can resurrect or clothe itself in our bodies, for although as individuals we die, 'our names are written in heaven' and we are resurrected or recreated.

In the **parable of the vineyard** it is not what work people do that earns them a reward. Everyone who turns up for work earns the same reward – salvation and eternal life. Their free will is what saves them and what the owner rewards. The robber on the cross next to Jesus earns paradise by his humility alone – by his own free will or choice to admit his own failure and his need for help. He has not one good work to offer and will be unable to do so now. In the **parable of the wedding feast** the people who are invited (a reference to the Jew's belief they were the 'chosen' people) are too arrogant to turn up. Their places are offered to complete strangers in the street (i.e anyone and everyone who can pass the test of humility). The Kingdom and its sharing of a common self are often described as a wedding feast. The people who are accepted into the wedding in this story are the ones who are wearing the correct clothes – the 'clothes of humility'. These are the ones who know they need grace or help in the shared person of the Holy Spirit. Those who think that they already have achieved the Kingdom or have been chosen because of their good works, morality or adherence to religious principles do not look for help (salvation) and so do not find the Kingdom.

Jesus teaches the principle of maintaining humility within **stories of wakefulness or awareness**. Grace (the Holy Spirit) is a state or person in which the prodigal Son is involved or partakes in, along with the Father. The humble prodigal Son must therefore be in a constant state of awareness or preparedness. The prodigal Son is no longer the 'innocent', unaware and faithful son but, just as he is constantly and consciously aware of his inheritance in the Kingdom, he must be aware of his constant need for help. The attitude that Jesus uses to describe this state is that of a servant – aware of his master and His needs at all times. In the **parable of the ten virgins**, it is those who do not keep enough oil in their lamps who miss the arrival of the bridegroom and fail to let him in. Again grace is perceived as a 'marriage' or coming together of the free wills of the Father and Son. If the son or servant is asleep or 'not there' when the master, or bridegroom, comes knocking, then he is not there to share in the 'feast' – the Kingdom of Heaven. He misses out on grace.

Jesus does not portray grace or relationship with the Father in the Holy Spirit as one of helplessness. The prodigal Son's humility earns him a complete share in the Kingdom. The good (humble) servant is given 'all that the Father has'. To be a good servant he must know all about the Father and all His needs. The Father listens to the prodigal or aware Son – as a loving Father. The Father does not dictate but listens. Only arrogance on the part of the prodigal Son, and his refusal to talk to and listen to the Father, exclude him from a relationship with the Father – and the grace offered by the shared person of the Holy Spirit. Prayer is a function of the prodigal Son's consciousness or awareness of his separation from the Father and his need for a relationship in the shared Holy Spirit – the need for grace and help. Jesus' reaction to all difficulties was humility and prayer.

Jesus described the power of grace in miracles. He showed that the power lay within us, not outside us – in our own humility. Jesus showed that grace was not a mighty hand that overturns the laws of Nature in order to save us. Grace is a humble involvement as prodigal Sons in an activity or event through our shared conviction, intuition or instinct in the Holy Spirit with the Father. The event is not supernatural but has such far reaching consequences as to be wondrous – something that makes all the difference to our lives. Miracles are mundane (worldly) but are things we know we, as arrogant prodigal Sons, could never have achieved on our own – by the prodigal mind, heart, body or will alone.

Jesus defined grace as always a sign that we, as prodigal humble Sons, are loved and a part of the Kingdom or God's self. The **story of the Good Samaritan** is given as an example of how mundane but important grace is. The man is stripped, robbed, beaten and left to die by the roadside. Many pious people from his own tribe walk on by for fear of meeting the robbers. A Samaritan (the most closed of tribes, in terms of customs and culture of the time) came by. He stooped, comforted, and tended to him. He put him on his donkey and took him to a public house and gave money to the landlord so that he might care for him until he was back on his feet. It was an anonymous gesture, so with no prospect of a reward, recognition or gain for the Samaritan of any kind. The help that the Samaritan gave him was minimal (he did not even personally take care of him), but to the victim it was all he needed – a helping hand to put him back onto his feet where he was before he was attacked. This is the same as the will or help (Holy Spirit) of the Father – He gives what we need to get us on our way, whatever the way might be.

Jesus describes the narrow gate of humility as a treasure beyond worldly price, for it leads us to the Helper, grace, the

Fathers' love and so eternal life. He asks, "What does it profit a man that he gains the world but loses his soul?". The price is the same as all creation. He rebukes the rich man for storing riches on earth where robbers can steal them from him and yet he neglects his soul – God's self within, and fails to 'store up riches in heaven'. He is not advocating poverty but warns people of thinking that storing wealth will save and protect us. Jesus asks people to safeguard our humility at all costs. He tells a **story of a man who finds a treasure** in a field. He sells all he has and buys the field. He asks for any prosperity we have to be used for the glorification of the Trinity that lies within us. In another story Jesus tells of a servant who works all day and when his master returns in the evening he cooks and serves his meal and only after he has done all for the master does he eat himself at the end of the day. The servant is safeguarding his master at all costs, because he knows the master's wealth is his wealth and the master's health is his health. Jesus goes even further in his teaching of the meaning of commitment to the common self or Kingdom of Heaven. He tells people to 'cut off your hand or pluck out your eye if it offends you. For it is better to enter the Kingdom of Heaven without a hand or an eye than not enter at all'. This is again a reference to the preciousness of the Kingdom and its grace. Without it we are doomed anyway to oblivion. His reference to the hand or eye is a metaphorical reference to things that are dear to us that separate us from our humility and so the Trinity or Kingdom within. If something will not allow us to be humble, then we must rid ourselves of it – even if it is something as important as our eye or right hand. Grace and eternal life are more important, and more useful to us, than even an eye or right hand. Jesus is referring to all the temptations that make us arrogant – ambitions, talents we possess, loved ones and family. They are not good or bad things per se, but are made bad or good by our arrogance or humility, as prodigal or aware Sons.

Jesus portrays salvation not just as a personal quest but a collective quest. The salvation of one person is there for all to share in. Our wealth is a common wealth. This is the message in the **story of the Talents.** Our salvation counts for nothing unless it has been shared. Jesus views his own salvation in these terms by saying, "where the carcass lies, the vultures shall gather". It is also at the heart of the communion of bread and wine where he shares his salvation with the world with the words, "This is my body. This is my blood (heart)". Each person's salvation is important only for what it contributes to the salvation of all Mankind – everybody. In the **story of the Good Shepherd** the shepherd goes in search of his lost sheep (leaving all the others in the open and vulnerable) not just because the sheep is individually precious, but because he is precious to the whole flock. So Jesus portrays salvation as a common commodity when he tells the **story of the Bad Manager.** This story is a message to the priests of the church, his apostles, but is also relevant to everyone who seeks to invest in salvation or the Kingdom. It roots the purpose of salvation, as a door to the Kingdom, which is the **sharing** of love, not righteousness. There is a master who calls his manager to him to have an account of his estate. The manager confesses that the master is owed a great debt by many people. The master tells his manager that he will be thrown into a prison, where he will stay until all the debt is paid, unless he can recover his money. The manager goes out to the master's debtors and gets them to pay that part of their debt that they are able to. The manager returns to the master and hands him the money he has been able to collect. The master is perversely accepting of the outcome. The master has recovered some of his estate, the manager has escaped prison from which there could be no release and he has made friends with his master's debtors. He has made 'friends in heaven'. The point that Jesus makes here is that it is better to make a spiritual compromise (just as it is to make a business compromise) rather than everyone end up a loser. In this story the master is God the Father and the manager is the priest of the prodigal Sons (the debtors). The priest fails to get from people their true debt to God the Father – the belief, faith and trust He deserves or has invested in them. If the priest tries to get people to hand over the full value of this debt without compromise, he knows he will return to the Father with nothing. The master knows this, so accepts the manager's compromise. The priest saves himself from rejection by the master and the debtors too – so the debtors are grateful to the manager when they find out that the master has accepted what they offered and they achieve acceptance, grace and the Kingdom of Heaven. Again Jesus is not interested in people's works, morality or tears of repentance (payments) – only that their humility and their knowledge that whatever they do it is not the true value of the debt they owe. It is this knowledge that is the real key or 'narrow gate' to the Kingdom of Heaven. The bad manager redeems his failure not by collecting the full value of the master's debt but by collecting some of the debt and so the debtors' admission of the true value of their debt – their collective knowledge or humility.

Jesus' life, from the moment of being born again (into the knowledge of humility), is a relentless and inevitable walk to this death by crucifixion. He is in full knowledge that the knowledge of the Kingdom of Heaven (the narrow gate), will be rejected, not just by the authorities but by Mankind – except his disciples. He has to leave a vivid and lasting imprint of the Kingdom of Heaven (the Trinity of God's self) behind him and by his physical death reveal that this Kingdom, self or Spirit is ubiquitous and eternal and lives in every person. It cannot be killed, for it has been always there within, is there and shall be there forevermore.

So the story unfolds as a revelation of the Trinity itself. John the Baptist, a born again prodigal body, a visionary of the mind of God is symbolically beheaded. Jesus, a born again prodigal mind, the 'Lamb' or heart of God, is symbolically spread eagled on a cross and his torso pierced with a spear. Water (a symbol of Truth) not blood pours from inside him. Jesus hands on the Trinity or Keys to the kingdom of Heaven to Peter, a prodigal heart, and he is martyred (gives witness to it) and crucified upside down like a piece of meat, symbolising the body of God.

John the Baptist inspires Jesus and hands to him his vision of a baptism of fire. Jesus hands this fire to Peter and tells him to 'feed my sheep'.

We see Jesus win the mind, heart and fellowship of many; Romans, Pharisees and people of all race and creed. He also makes real enemies. We see him, as he predicted, cause a divide, "I have not come not to bring peace but a sword (of Truth). Brother shall be set against brother, mother against daughter..." Jesus is bringing something radical to Man and he knows it is, as all Truth, something that can only be rejected or accepted. We have the free will to believe and see it, or not. It is the kind of Truth which we see or believe simply of our free will or desire alone. If we do not want it we shall be blinded by our own will. "Those who are not with me are against me ... Those who are not against me are with me". It is a Truth that describes itself purely as a person or Trinity of Love, so will never compromise the principle of free will. This is what Jesus calls the Holy Spirit (person of free will) the spirit of Truth, a person 'who will lead Mankind into all of the Truth'. The Holy Spirit and its Truth will only respond to the wills of the Father and Son. We do not see the Holy Spirit if it is our will not to see it.

In the story there is a moment where Jesus invites a few disciples, his inner cabinet if you like, to a secluded place in the mountains to pray. He takes Peter (a prodigal heart), James (a prodigal mind) who is possibly his brother and John (a prodigal body). Days before the meeting, Jesus asks his disciples, "Who do people say I am?" They reply that some think he is John the Baptist; some Elijah; some say he is one of the prophets. He then asks them, "Who do you think I am?" They reply that they think he is the Christ or Messiah. Jesus chooses a small intimate meeting to confirm in himself and his disciples his identity. It is naturally a private and intimate moment for it involved a deep profound, personal and emotional experience for those present – a sharing of the Truth that God's self or the Kingdom dwells with Man. Jesus becomes radiant, his clothes blinding white and he talks with the spirits of Moses and Elijah. It is called the **Transfiguration** because it is the moment that a group of people first share in and experience the reality of a common self or God's self within Man. The Kingdom within Jesus shines out for them to see. The disciples would have appeared to see these spirits as a consequence of the actual reality of Jesus meeting them within himself – in the Kingdom. This act of talking to others serves to reveal the commonality of the Kingdom within. Because the self is a common self, physical death is not a barrier within it. The change in Jesus would have been dramatic and it would have infected the disciples emotionally too. They would have seen him in their mind's eye as radiant in every sense, including the light around him. It would have been something like the effect of being in love has on a person's perception of someone. They glow and the object of our love can even appear God like. Jesus here is confirming in himself physically the presence of God's self (Kingdom) within himself and all people – and the disciples can see it. The spiritual creates its own reality or 'body' which is as real as the wine was in Cana. The disciples are enveloped in a 'cloud of confusion' and they hear a voice declare that 'Jesus is the Son of God and that they should listen to him'. Jesus is transfigured into the living entity of God's self in the eyes of these disciples. The significance of this event is that the Kingdom of Heaven or self of God can and does express itself through anything and everything in creation. Peter wants to build 'shelters' for Jesus, John the Baptist and Elijah – ever the prodigal heart. They are natural church builders. In the words of Churchill, also a prodigal heart, 'we shape our buildings so that they might shape us'.

Jesus makes a triumphant entry into Jerusalem, as if he were truly an earthly king, with the populace throwing palm fronds into the road before him. Jesus symbolically rides a donkey, the transport of the lowliest in society, hinting that his kingship is 'not of this world'. There is almost a hint of deliberate pantomime here, a poking of fun at the worldly concept of kingship, and we can also feel Jesus having a little private joke at the expense of the Pharisees. Here Jesus is making the point that he has not come to set up a Christian government, law, state, society, religion or church fellowship. He has come to bring the Truth, Life and Way of his followers into this world. His followers are asked to render what is of this world (Caesar's) to this world (Caesar) and to God what is God's. There can be no institutions in this world that can mirror the Kingdom of Heaven. He says later to his tormentors – "My kingdom is not of this world". It is a kingship that lies within all people. Jesus has not come to establish a prodigal Kingship. He knows his popularity will be a further nail in his coffin. The authorities were galvanized to get rid of him. Jesus finishes the 'job', by purposefully entering the very sanctum of government and religious authority and attacking their corruption and hypocrisy by literally beating the moneylenders out of the Temple. The Temple was the seat of religious authority and Jewry. He had repeatedly sniped at and exposed the hypocrisy of the Pharisees and the people in control. This act sealed his fate and Jesus knew it.

At the Last Supper Jesus sums up his mission to his disciples. It is a poignant moment when he brings all the disciples together to say 'goodbye'. It is where he physically binds them into a fellowship with a simple ceremony of communion based on his own example. He asks them "to love one another as I have loved you" – i.e. with humility. He binds all his future followers in this simple and ubiquitous ceremony – the sharing of wine and bread. The bread and wine are symbolic of the body/fellowship and heart of the shared self of God, which lies in all people – the Kingdom of the Father, Son and Holy Spirit.

Here primarily Jesus declares that he is to be handed over to the authorities or betrayed by one of the disciples. He points to who it is by dipping his bread into his soup and handing it to Judas. He tells Judas to 'go and do what he has to do'. The bread is symbolic of Jesus handing over his body to Judas. There has been an agreed plan but only Jesus knows the outcome – his death. Jesus warns everyone of this outcome when he infers that Judas will be blamed for it. "Better that man never be born". He is warning of Judas' forthcoming remorse, isolation, and inevitable suicide. Even with this act of handing Judas some bread, no-one suspects or can believe Judas is the betrayer or the nature of his plan. This is because Judas is the trusted confidante and assistant of Jesus and they know that Judas loves Jesus. Judas, with Jesus' approval, has hatched a plan to save Jesus' life by bargaining with the authorities. Jesus will be taken unharmed and given a fair trial if Judas leads the authorities to him. Judas believes that Jesus will not be condemned if given a fair hearing. Jesus will surely be assassinated by hired killers otherwise.

Jesus retires to the garden of Gethsemane with the disciples. He prays not for the world but for his disciples and thanks the Father for keeping them safe and in the faith. The disciples are tired and soon fall asleep and Jesus is left alone in the dark with his fears and doubts. The garden is symbolic of the Holy Spirit (like the vineyard) and Jesus experiences abandonment, in this dark garden, of fellowship. As a prodigal mind his Father is in the heart and Holy Spirit in the fellowship. He experiences abandonment of both the prodigal fellowship (of the disciples) and that of the Father. He walks over to the disciples and rebukes them for falling asleep, and then returns to his own loneliness, fear and doubt. We see Jesus agonize with his prodigal self. He is visited by the snake. He momentarily loses his belief and is unsure of his strength to carry the message of the Trinity to the end. He literally sweats blood, a recognised medical condition that involves the bursting of capillaries in the sweat glands that can occur under great emotional stress. He asks the Father if he really has to go through with the torture and death he knows is coming. "Let this cup pass from me". He receives strength in his body and fellowship from 'angels' – the help of the Holy Spirit and he agrees to go on.

Judas arrives. Earlier he tells his disciples after the Last Supper to bring swords. Once he told them to go out and spread the gospel, with no money and only the clothes they wore. Jesus asked them if they had lacked anything. They replied that they did not and God provided all they needed. Now he told them to go home and get swords and arm themselves. They managed to get together a couple of swords. When the soldiers came, it was part of the Judas' plan to protect Jesus from harm, by identifying him with a kiss. As the soldiers stepped forward to arrest Jesus, Peter hacked at a soldier and cut his ear. Jesus stopped Peter's attack and gave healing to the soldier. He warned Peter that, "blood begets blood". Violence breeds violence. However Jesus was not a pacifist. He had after all used extreme violence against the traders and money lenders in the Temple. He however was showing his disciples that, whether Christianity had to fight wars or not, it did not depend on either pacifism or war to defend itself. It would, as the Truth, prevail by merely the fact it was the Truth, Life and the Way. Jesus is purposefully ambivalent about pacifism and war. The Holy Spirit will lead people in the decision as to how defend itself and they had to be open to it.

Jesus is passive throughout his trial. He does not offer a defence and says very little, frustrating anybody's attempts to incriminate him. He constantly answers questions directed at him with a question. For example when asked if he is the Son of God he replies, "It is you who say I am". As a result neither Herod, the puppet king of the Romans nor Pilate, the Roman governor, can find any reason to convict Jesus. He exposes the lies and false accusations of his accusers by directing them back at them.

So Jesus, in the end, is not convicted on any legal evidence but by the will of the people (symbolic of Mankind) who want Barabas, a Zionist and a murderer, released. He is the people's real hero because he actually led a rebellion against the Romans. Herod sees Jesus as no real threat to him and his position and makes fun of him. Pilate is under pressure from Rome to keep the Jews from rising up and so goes with the will of the people. He washes his hands of the affair, finding no fault with Jesus himself. So we see Jesus led to his death as a joke figure. He has not been convicted of anything or proved himself to be either a brave revolutionary or a supernatural Son of God. He is standing helpless, forlorn and friendless, being laughed at, wearing a King's robe jokingly donated by Herod (who treated him as a harmless fool to be whipped and set free). Jesus ends up on his knees like a grotesque pantomime figure of a king with a crown of thorns, being beaten and mocked. He becomes an awful, empty figure of failure – failure as a heroic revolutionary or Messiah, as a Son of God or Christ (the anointed one) and as the spiritual king of the Jews. His followers must have turned away in embarrassment. He had entered Jerusalem a few days earlier to join the Passover, as a king with people crying, 'Bless him in the name of the Lord' and throwing palms in his path. From these heights he had sunk to a friendless and pitiful joke. Jesus had to endure this utter humiliation and watch how the decent people now viewed him – with pity and embarrassment; a joke that went horribly wrong; a mistake; some crazy man or deluded person who did not deserve such a punishment. Others, less decent, saw him as a failed Messiah who had let them down and they heaped scorn and abuse on him. The Pharisees and their cronies wanted Jesus to suffer as an example to others who might want to challenge their privilege and authority.

Just a few amongst the crowd maybe felt guilt that deep down, in all truth, they had in fact let Jesus down. They might have felt unease at putting even a failed Messiah to death. People were very superstitious and rumours and paranoia could spread like wild fire. There would have been rumours of predictions surrounding Jesus' death, not least his claim of his own resurrection. Very ordinary happenings soon become exaggerated and extraordinary, as people's imaginations are gripped by fear and superstition. Jesus' life ended in a similar way to how it began; with an event whose great expectation was only matched by its apparent insignificance.

On the Via Dolorosa Jesus was comforted and supported by three individuals. They each represent the comfort of the mind, heart and body of God by Man. Veronica steps forward and mops Jesus' brow with the fabric of her veil. This is symbolic of Veronica helping Jesus with his vision (belief) of the Trinity, and so he can see the road ahead. Mary, his mother, is reputed to have stepped forward when he is pinned to the ground by his cross and encouraged him saying, "I am here" and urging him onward. This is symbolic of Mary helping Jesus find courage (heart) in his mission of the Trinity. Thirdly Simon of Cyrene is ordered by a Roman soldier to help the exhausted Jesus with his cross. This is symbolic of helping Jesus, by giving him fellowship and strength, with the weight of his mission to reveal the Trinity.

Jesus goes to his crucifixion as the Father, humble prodigal Son and Holy Spirit – the three persons as one. The humble prodigal Son does the will of the Father and the Father loves the Son and the person of the Holy Spirit fulfils the will of both as one will. All struggle to the crucifixion and experience death. The Son relies more and more heavily on the Father and the Father on the Son, in the person of the Holy Spirit. Each draws on the other to the point of annihilation. As the life in Jesus ebbs away to the point of annihilation, Jesus cries out in desperation, "Father, Father why have you abandoned me?" For a moment Jesus appears to be left alone and abandoned as the Son, without the Father and so the help of the Holy Spirit. He manages to say in his dying breath, "Into Your hands I commend my spirit". He has lost all except the Son's will which he commends to the Father in the Holy Spirit.

Why did Jesus feel abandoned? There are three reasons. In the self of Jesus (as in all of us) God experienced the crucifixion in three ways. Firstly he experienced it as the Father. God the Father experienced Himself every bit of scorn, every lash of the whip, every humiliation and the rejection of Himself by the whole of Mankind. He had opened His heart fully to Mankind, which is what He does, and He had been totally rejected. At the end of the crucifixion the Father was in no better shape than the Son to respond to his call. The Father felt annihilated too.

Secondly God the Son experienced every bit of suffering too.

The Son was dying along with the Father. Jesus was not just the singular perfectly humble prodigal Son of God but a representative of the whole of prodigal Mankind. The Father was helpless Himself and could not help the Son who had volunteered to become a symbol of the whole of Mankind. Jesus did not stand aside from Mankind but offered himself up as a symbol of all Mankind – all Man's prodigal nature. Instead of condemning Mankind he pleaded its case before the Father – "Father, forgive them for they do not know what they do". Jesus was offering to the stricken Father not just himself but was asking for His help on behalf of all Mankind.

Thirdly, as explained above, God the Holy Spirit was also experiencing the crucifixion and annihilation. Jesus carried by his own will, or on account of his own humility, the case for the forgiveness of all Mankind. He was offering up, in his own person, all the prodigal sin and rejection of the Father by Mankind in the shared Holy Spirit. It is no surprise that the Father's will or love in the Holy Spirit should have recoiled heartbroken.

So we have a Father dying rejected alongside His Son and that same Son asking for the forgiveness of all Mankind from that same Father. For one dark moment Jesus is caught between the rejection of both the Father and Mankind; a child waiting in hope alone for the forgiveness of his father. The psychology of this moment is the moment when Mankind becomes aware of the infinite intractable sinfulness of Original Sin (or his becoming an aware Son) in the person of the prodigal Son, and the infinite forgiveness of the Father. The infinite forgiveness of the Father (and so the redemption of grace) is only found by the prodigal Son by his own admission of this infinite sin – his infinite humility in the shared person of the Holy Spirit or Helper. This infinite humility of will in the spirit of Love (Holy Spirit) is exactly what we see in Jesus when he accepts even the abandonment of the Father's spirit of Love, with the words, "Into Your hands I commend my spirit (the spirit of prodigal Mankind)".

From now on, the Spirit of humility alone in the prodigal Son grants him grace and forgiveness. It also shows the ability of the Son to stand alone without the Father or more accurately, in the form of Jesus, to stand in for the Father. Jesus reveals the Son, prodigal or not, to have the same capacity (share of the Kingdom) as the Father and therefore to be worthy still of the Kingdom. The psychological significance of Jesus' act of crucifixion to Mankind is to establish that the act of Original Sin (becoming aware) has to be forgivable. Jesus presents the absolute humility of the prodigal Son (on behalf of all Mankind) before the Father in or through the shared person of the Holy Spirit. If the Father turns away and condemns the prodigal Son and his state and does not grant him unconditional Love, forgiveness and help, then there can be no sharing with the Father in the Holy Spirit, no grace with the Father, no help from the Father, no entry into the Kingdom, no sharing in God's self, no eternal life in that self, no hope of resurrection. The prodigal Son and so Mankind will be doomed to just a pointless prodigal existence, his own selfish illusions and devices and oblivion.

Although there are various accounts of unnatural happenings occurring when Jesus died, it was a very inauspicious and common death. Nobody came to save him as expected. The fact that the curtain of the Temple was torn is not dramatic – an unconvincing report of an earthquake and darkness falling over the land. It all smacks of a general shock at the realization that this miracle worker was no more than a human, and people looked for more. They did not still understand the significance of what he had revealed. They did not understand that he had revealed something that lay within them – they were still looking outwards. Everyone who loved him would have suffered an appalling sense of emptiness. Before he died Jesus would have witnessed the bewilderment and confusion of all those who loved him. And he would have been helpless to explain any further his mission. He would have suffered an agony in leaving them in such a state of confusion, bewilderment and demoralisation. As he died the enormity of his personal sacrifice on this cross was juxtaposed, only feet away, by the enormity of the people's misunderstanding.

Jesus, on more than one occasion, hints to the disciples that he will be raised from the dead. They naturally feel that it will be a physical resurrection like they believed they saw with Lazarus. He talks of 'this temple being torn down and rebuilt in three days'. This claim becomes common knowledge and passes as a rumour about the Messiah. People would have greeted such a claim much as the claim of lotteries. We know the odds of winning are effectively impossible but are blinded to the fact by our hope. We are fascinated and drawn by the tiny possibility, simply because the prize is so enormous.

Jesus actually tells people that in heaven people are 'as angels'. They have spiritual bodies. These bodies have no physical basis anymore than the spiritual Trinity within us does. If you dissect a body you will not find the Father, Son and Holy Spirit but we can see it is present. This Trinity or God's self has a mind, heart and body and we witness its presence in its effects – in those who witness to it. It is the same as the 'spiritual wine' in Cana. People taste, see and experience wine because they believe in the idea or spirit of wine. So it is with the resurrection of Jesus in these early days three days after his death. His 'believers' see, feel and experience the presence of his powerful Spirit or self, until he fades away. This resurrection is not the same as the resurrection at the end of time but a grief response of those who experienced him, were close to him and loved him. When their grief faded the apparitions faded. It does not however make their experience any less significant or real – like the wine at Cana. The resurrection to eternal life at the end of time is a wholly different event and begins symbolically with the resurrection of Jesus the man. Jesus calls this his 'second coming'. His resurrection is assured – 'he sits on the right hand of God the Father'. People who believe in the Trinity within are resurrected by God's self to share in God's self, Trinity or Kingdom. The reason Jesus 'lives' on, but is not seen, is because he encapsulates the Spirit of the Trinity and this is ubiquitous and eternal in all people. It lives in all of us now, always has and always will.

The physical resurrection of a loved one is a natural and enormous urge in the bereft. People want to believe that they have not died and left them alone. It is not uncommon for grieving people to 'see' the dead and even have tactile sensations with the dead. The disciples were married to Jesus. They had given up their lives to follow him and knew him intimately. His extraordinary impact on them was not going to stop with his physical death. Jesus knew this and could safely say that he would live on and appear to them in their grief. He said to them that he, the temple (his body), would be torn down and rebuilt in three days. He would appear to them after his death. Neurologists call this phenomenon a 'crisis apparition'. It is the 'body of belief' – spirit made real. Spiritual wine. As in Cana Jesus had taught people that belief has 'flesh and bones' or a reality.

The third day has a special significance in this process of grief. It is on the third day that the crisis of bereavement reaches its climax and it is realised that the person is physically dead and not returning. The experience of the dead person's spirit or self is brought into a sharp focus and can come to 'life' by its presence (belief) within people alone. Likewise it is on the third day that a mother fully realises the physical birth of the self of a child and the 'baby blues' set in. It constitutes an emotional moment, when maybe she feels the guilt and sadness of bringing a being into a world of prodigal suffering and death. Also the mother maybe feels the full implications of the loss of her own freedom and independence.

Jesus emulated a common self of Man, God's self. He therefore also emulated a Spirit or person that could recognizably live on in anyone who accepted the presence of this Spirit or person within them. He is therefore reported to have taken the form of a stranger (other people). The spirit or person of Jesus became therefore the Spirit or person of a common self we all share – God's self. This is what Christians today mean when they talk of believing in Jesus. It is an invitation simply to believe that we all have within us (and always have had) God's self, the Trinity or the Kingdom of Heaven. Nothing more.

The chief priests had a guard mounted on the tomb for the three days to prevent the followers of Jesus taking the body and claiming he had risen from the dead, which would have increased his followers even more. After the tomb was found empty, the priests met with the elders and bribed the soldiers with a large sum of money to say that the disciples had taken the body while they were asleep (as if they had known this if they were asleep). The Roman governor would believe them and they would be let off the hook. The priests would have seen the governor as well no doubt! It would be highly likely that the followers of Jesus could have bribed the soldiers for the body too, with an equally large sum of money. They may have wanted to hide his body for one very good reason. The country was in turmoil and the authorities feared trouble of any kind. Jesus had created trouble and had been executed for subversion. His followers would have realised that his tomb could become a focus of worship and subversion and so a threat to the authorities. They may have wished to take the body before the authorities did, if the authorities had not already. The disciples went into hiding after the theft of the body had been discovered. This theft, either by Jesus' followers or the authorities would have been done without the family's consent, who if they knew would have led people inevitably to the hidden location. If the guards took money from the priests, they would equally have been prepared to take it from Jesus' followers – and neither wanted Jesus' resting place to be public property for their own reasons.

Jesus represented a love and hope beyond words. As he expressed it himself, 'a light had gone from the world'. There was suddenly no hope, no love, no power – nothing. To use Jesus' words, "the sheep were scattered". The disciples must have wondered what on earth they were doing together. It cannot be underestimated how much spiritual devastation Jesus' death brought in its wake – an unimaginable sense of loss in every sense.

The first to see Jesus' spirit is Mary Magdalene. This is not surprising as she loved Jesus the most of all as her saviour and no doubt as a man too. She loved him in all ways – spiritually, emotionally and physically. Jesus said this in his lifetime, when she wept at his feet – that the most fallen in spirit are the most grateful for their restoration. Such love made the disciples uneasy. She had gone in the dark to the tomb to grieve; the most heartbroken and lost of all – and the closest to Jesus. She found that 'they had taken Jesus' body and the tomb was empty'. She called the disciples and there would have been pandemonium in the dark with the caretaker, guards and maybe the perpetrators too. She is distressed and sees Jesus, thinking him to be the gardener. He says to her, "Do not hold onto me, because I have not yet gone to the Father". The spirit or person of Jesus is declaring itself to Mary that it is his spirit and not flesh. Jesus knew Mary would have an overwhelming desire to fall into Jesus' arms – make his spirit physically real. The spirit of Jesus is wisely preventing Mary from conjuring up a 'flesh and blood' Jesus to which she would cling, and try to draw back from the grave in a desperate and futile gesture. Jesus' spirit disappears and Mary runs to tell the disciples what she has seen.

Now Jesus appears a number of times to a number of groups of his disciples. News would have travelled fast of Mary's experience. Jesus' spirit becomes alive in the disciples' lives, giving them hope, comfort and guidance, of the sort that he gave them while he was alive. They would have begun to recall his words, summarise his life and spirit (as often he told them they would). He warned them he would die and it was part of the plan. He told them that this would not be the end and he would be 'raised up'. He told them he would rebuild his temple and so 'appear' to them after his death. He told them he would send them his spirit and that he would be with them always. He told them that when two or more were gathered in his name (person, spirit or Holy Spirit), he would be there and all that they asked would be given. He told them always to be a part of the vine (a part of the Holy Spirit). All that his life signified and all that he had been as a man would have started to come back to them and reform. Sooner or later their minds would have put 'flesh and bones and senses' to this spirit of Jesus. They would simply find after his death that his spirit (the Holy Spirit) was within them, to be resurrected by them. He appears before them behind locked doors in the evening of the third day after the burial, while they hide from the authorities. They no doubt had been sharing memories, feelings and longings about him in the gloom. He breathes the Holy Spirit onto them. This is a description of the moment where those who are present realise that the spirit or person of Jesus is the person of the Holy Spirit. They are truly 'born again in the spirit' now as Jesus wanted them to be. They realise that the person of the Father, Son and Holy Spirit are all the same person, and is also the self of Man and so within Man. Those present are discovering and sharing the experience of Jesus and the Trinity he represented within them, but they sense it is 'breathed' into them. They feel they are letting the Holy Spirit into themselves – a common experience of being born again. In fact this person or self was always within them. They feel the power and presence of Jesus (literally as an apparition before them) and all he represented, not outside them but inside them. It is a new feeling, a liberating and empowering feeling. They are filled with relief and joy. It is a turning point in their grief, an affirming experience. Jesus said he would return but they had not understood how; but now they could feel and even see him. This feeling of being filled with or reunited with the spirit of a departed loved one is often the moment when people feel they can pick themselves off the floor and move forward in that spirit – however shakily.

Jesus appears to Thomas who has doubted the others' story about Jesus' appearance to them. Thomas is still in denial of what he sees and so also of the spirit that is within him, the vision of Jesus. This spirit of Jesus within asks him to feel the wounds of his hands to prove it is really here with him. Thomas is the arch prodigal mind and so the unbeliever or 'doubter'. His prodigal mind stops him believing in the presence and power of the spirit or person of God within himself. His heart has faith in Jesus but his mind disbelieves. Because he does not believe in the 'wine' he cannot taste the 'wine'. Jesus' spirit asks him to touch his wounds. Thomas puts his hand into the wounds and can feel the body of Jesus. Thomas realises or believes that this spirit within him is real. His belief puts flesh and blood onto this spirit or person of Jesus within him. Jesus had demonstrated that he had become alive in them, so alive to them. This is what he meant when he said he would come alive again – in them. Jesus tells them that they are lucky that they knew him in life and so believed in his spirit. Many would come after them who would never know him but still they would believe in him and he would be alive in them. There is a measure of humility dished out to the disciples here explaining that the best is yet to come. Jesus is reported to have left through a wall proving without doubt that he was not flesh and bone in a physical sense but a spiritual body.

Jesus appears again on the shore of Lake Tiberius. Seven disciples have been fishing all night and have caught nothing. They are interestingly remaining together in hope and have not gone back to their homes. They have obeyed Jesus' call to stay together and wait for something to happen, some guidance. They were uncertain and in limbo and still missing Jesus. They had failed to catch fish – a great downer for people so reliant on the sea for their livelihood. Jesus had so often provided for them with his instinct and intuition. They were tired from grief and work. Then someone shouts from the shore and tells them where to cast their nets, and they catch a net full. It is like old times again. One of them recognises the man is Jesus. The disciple who 'saw' this man as Jesus recognised the man Jesus by his actions and behaviour rather than his face. The spirit of a person is more recognisable, if not entirely so, by his manner, not his features. They go ashore and there is a fire with fish and bread. The man asks them to bring some of the fish they have caught. Here was the spirit of Jesus feeding them, looking after them, but there is no immediate physical recognition of Jesus. The disciple who recognised him (most probably a prodigal body) falls silent now. There is no greeting, embracing or expressions of joy. They dare not talk to this man who is not physically Jesus, but filled with the spirit of Jesus or the Holy Spirit. Finally this man speaks and asks Peter to reaffirm his love for Jesus three times. He confirms again his wish for Peter to build his church and 'feed his sheep'. In this culture such a repetition three times makes a promise eternally binding. Peter now loves Jesus not as the man but as the spirit of God (The Father, Son and Holy Spirit) that he represented. He affirms his self as having been born again in the spirit of God. Peter then makes a gesture towards the disciple that Jesus 'loved' – his favourite. There is a natural conjecture that this might be his brother James (a prodigal mind like himself) or John who was a confidante like Judas (a prodigal body who most understood the Truth) or even Mary Magdalene. The point though is that Jesus was a man who had physical attractions (including of a sexual nature) and people would have been aware of the 'chemistry' of his relationships. There would have been insecurity and confusion in the disciples, spoken or unspoken, as how to proceed with Jesus' legacy and who should lead. Peter asks what is to become of this 'favourite'. Jesus is firm and tells him to 'mind his own business' and do his job. He will take care of the one he loves. Jesus is saying that the business of the Kingdom of Heaven comes first, as it did in his life.

The purpose of this meeting is to confirm Peter, not so much as a leader, but a rallying point for all people – this is what 'feed my sheep' means. All people have God's self within them but Peter is to put it altogether into a fellowship based on one premise only – the common humility of the prodigal Son as demonstrated by Jesus. He must dress this up as food so people may eat it. The **'stranger on the shore'** would have known Jesus, followed him, been filled with the Holy Spirit and imparted therefore the will of this spirit to the disciples – and the disciples recognised it as such.

Jesus describes the strength of this spirit, embodied by his spirit, and present in all Mankind, by saying, "I was, am and shall be forevermore". His spirit is ubiquitous and eternal. There are therefore more emotional sightings of this spirit (as Jesus) over the next few weeks as news spreads of its presence abroad. On the **road to Emmaus** a stranger again joins two of Jesus' followers as they walk along and instructs them (which felt like a fire burning within them), stays with them and shares a meal, only revealing himself as Jesus before immediately disappearing from sight. They only recognise him when they see him break bread, again suggesting that they recognised him only by his spirit or by his manner of speech and action. The experience of a burning fire within them describes the intensity of emotion within them. Passionate feelings, intensified by grief, do burn and almost sear us inside like molten liquid. It is a good description of the hope, love and fellowship that Jesus left behind in people. People had to grasp the vision of what he had revealed or lose it. They talk to the 'stranger' about what had happened to their Messiah and how he had not measured up to expectations – he had deserted them. There would have been a lot of soul searching, doubts and insecurities in such followers as these. Here we see, in this touching little drama, the spirit of Jesus or Holy Spirit rise up in one follower to help dispel the fears and doubts of others. His spirit clings desperately within people encouraging them to get up and respond to his eternal call – Follow me to the Kingdom.

These two followers are electrified by their 'helper' and burst in on the eleven disciples in Jerusalem and tell them what they have seen. Previously the disciples had been at a low ebb and doubting everything. Jesus had come to them again. After this outburst by the two from Emmaus, the spirit of Jesus appears again to these excited people. Again he encourages them not to doubt his spirit, the Holy Spirit. He challenges them to touch him and eats with them.

Each time the spirit appears to the disciples they are in disbelief and each time Jesus gets them to be bold in their belief. We see psychologically a group of people who have been fed a vision of self (the Trinity) that is 'unbelievable' or beyond the prodigal mind; a promise of eternal life, something that gives their lives a real meaning. This is the vision of God the Father, Son and Holy Spirit in all people, a love and peace beyond understanding (the prodigal mind), of unfailing help and grace. We see their struggle to maintain within themselves the momentum of belief, faith and trust, the reality of it all, begun by Jesus.

There is a last appearance by the spirit of Jesus, where all the disciples are present. His spirit makes them go all the way. He gets them to touch him and he eats with them. He is facially recognisable as Jesus. He consolidates in their minds the knowledge of the scriptures (their place in the story). This is a collective apparition and is a result of a revelation and confirmation of their collective belief. Without this absolute solidarity of belief in the Trinity and Kingdom, as described in the person or spirit of Jesus, this church will not float. It is an 'all or nothing' commitment and they know it. Everything Jesus said, did and represented was completely real or it was not. Their collective belief in the spirit of Jesus is so entrenched in them (like the wine in Cana) that they conjure a fully resurrected 'flesh and bones' relationship with him. They walk, eat and talk with him. A secret camera in the room would have recorded a bizarre behaviour, but it is a sign that they all have a common understanding and 'working' model of the Truth, Life and the Way, the Trinity of God's self – the Father, Son and Holy Spirit. They are prepared to receive permanently, as a fellowship or church of Mankind, that which Jesus promised – the Holy Spirit or Helper. His would give them the wherewithal to teach and spread the gospel to all of Mankind. They are calm and ready. Jesus leads them out of Jerusalem to Bethany. He blesses them, which is a touching reminder to them that he is pleased with them and they have done well. They are ready to go out on their own and a blessing (whether by a father or mother) is always a reminder to the son or daughter that they have all they need within them. It is a final affirmation of the relationship for the blesser and the blessed. It sets in stone, with the blessed's acceptance, the eternal relationship. Jesus tells the disciples to 'wait in the city until the power from above comes down upon you'. This is a reference to the full power of the Holy Spirit that will be needed to build the church and give them all the help they need.

Jesus' spirit now **'ascends into heaven'** and he is lost from sight forever, until his resurrection at the second coming at the end of time. It is natural for the disciples to see heaven in physical terms as 'up there' but spiritually it is a moment where Jesus' spirit fades within them and so the apparition of him disappears back into the Kingdom. A line is drawn and the disciples now are forced to turn their attention outwards from themselves. Their belief must now be directed not at conjuring up a flesh and bones image of Jesus the man but to putting flesh and bones to spirit within themselves, in others and the world. They have to go work. They worshipped Jesus and then went to the Temple in the city and 'spent all their time giving thanks to God'.

Jesus had said that 'the birds have their nests and the foxes have their holes but the Son of Man has nowhere to rest his head'. By this Jesus was explaining his unique situation. He was completely alone in his work. He had no fellowship of Man to take comfort from. It is also a reference to people of the Holy Spirit being free. As Sons of God believers do not have a physical home but a spiritual home or Kingdom that is eternal and endless. It is membership of a Kingdom of another world. They belong everywhere they go.

The disciples are now to spread this Kingdom everywhere. They have consolidated their fellowship of belief and passed through their grief. They even understand Judas' role in the story and Peter honours Judas when he declares 'Judas was a member of our group, for he was chosen to have a part in our work'. He decides that he should be replaced. There are 120 believers at this meeting and they vote for another disciple. Lots are drawn to choose between two candidates.

Pentecost is the event that is considered the birth of the Christian Church – the event horizon or point of no return. In the same way that the individual is born again in the spirit, Pentecost describes the moment Mankind was born again in the spirit. It occurred when the disciples and followers were celebrating Shavuot, a spring harvest festival (50 days into the year). There was a noise in the sky, which sounded like a strong wind blowing and it filled the whole house. They saw what looked like tongues of fire, which spread out and touched them. Everyone was filled with the Holy Spirit and began to talk in different languages. There was a collective revelation or participation of the openness and humility of the prodigal Son with the loving spirit of the Father in the Holy Spirit. The Holy Spirit therefore appeared in response to this humility with the love of the Father. The event was an external manifestation of what was **already** in the minds, hearts and fellowship of those gathered together. The Holy Spirit came alive in the congregation. The phenomenon of noise, light and voices was a consequence of the mass realization or revelation of the people. People watching saw only people who appeared drunk and possessed, but Peter said it was the Holy Spirit. People behaved and looked differently in the light of the revelation of the Holy Spirit, just as Jesus did during the Transfiguration. Three thousand people were brought into the faith after Peter's stirring speech about Jesus and his message. Jesus' message or Truth about the Trinity had an effect like a dam bursting. People behaved like an army of slaves suddenly given their freedom back and with it their worth. People were ecstatic with a new hope. They were given the tools (the Truth, Life and Way within them) to transform their personal lives and communities, through their own shared humility, the Father's love and the help of their shared Holy Spirit. Jesus had won back the Kingdom for them.

It was a feature of Jesus' message of the Truth, Life and Way that it behaved like fire. Jesus said he had come to earth to 'light a fire'. John the Baptist said Jesus would baptise 'with fire'. If a fire is not fed it will die. It cannot stand still. It grows and spreads by consuming or changing substances – by oxidation. It is a dramatic and colourful chemical reaction that depends on an input of energy as heat or a spark, which then produces heat and is sustained by the heat it produces. The behaviour of fire parallels the instigation, nature, maintenance and spread of faith. It appears to have a life of its own. John the Baptist heralded the spark who was Jesus. The disciples were consumed and changed producing more heat, which ignited the people and so it spread outwards. The heat of passion is a necessary ingredient and also a product of faith. The Christian faith spread explosively, like a wild fire, from the Pentecost with dramatic visions and miracles. 'People lived sharing everything with each other, praising God and enjoying the good will of all the people'. This sudden joyous birth of a community would be unmatched by the slow burn and adolescent stumbling of Christianity in later years.

Chapter Nine

The Future and Judgement

The Future

Jesus dealt with the natural concerns of his followers about the future. He wanted to reassure the disciples with a long term vision or strategy that they could hand on to the generations – a survival package.

Matthew 24 describes what Jesus does. The disciples had visited the Temple in Jerusalem and as they were leaving they remark on its beauty, as one of the largest and grandest buildings in the world. It would have been an icon of the prodigal world, a testimony to Man's power, rather like a huge natural wonder. Jesus had attacked the Pharisees and stirred up a hornets' nest, placing the movement and the disciples in danger. He knows he cannot return to the Temple and Jerusalem until his triumphant but fateful return on Palm Sunday. He knows the joyous welcome will quickly become a rejection and death. He is upset at this imminent rejection by Jerusalem's people. They represent the people of the world and he loves them. He blames Jerusalem and its authorities for this. His frustration is almost parental. He looks back at the city and says, "Jerusalem, Jerusalem! How many times have I wanted to put my arms around your people, just as a hen gathers her chicks under her wings, but you would not let me!" he says the Temple will be empty and abandoned as a result. He is explaining there will no Christian love in the city and its Temple. It will suffer as a result.

The disciples are perplexed and worried at Jesus' vision of the future of Jerusalem. If Jerusalem cannot be liberated or won over with the mighty Temple and its importance in the world, who can be? It made everyone nervous; hence the comment on its might and beauty. Jesus replies, "Yes, you may look at all these. I tell you this: not a single stone will be left in its place; every one of them will be thrown down." This is a reference to the impermanence of the world. The Temple is in fact destroyed later in an uprising against the Romans but Jesus is saying that it is not the might and beauty of the world that endures but the Word or spiritual life. This is understood by the disciples later and is why, when they are on the Mount of Olives, they seek Jesus out for a 'private meeting' to discuss their worries concerning the future.

Jesus has a sharp insight as to how the faith will develop and so is of great help to the disciples in terms of guidance, comfort, inspiration and encouragement, all the attributes of effective leadership. Firstly he warns his followers not to expect life to change after he has given his message to the world. Life will go on with natural disasters and wars all around. He averted both panic and depression by getting them to view these things as 'the birth pangs of a new creation'. This was designed to turn them away from falsely interpreting the events outside them and see all outside themselves as opportunities to grow the new creation within them.

Christians will appear to be losing ground, with all Mankind hating them. Evil will spread. Many Christians will give up their faith, betray each other and even hate each other. 'Such will be the spread of evil that many people's love will grow cold. Many false prophets will appear to lead people astray'. Jesus understood that his message of love would be hijacked by communities and nations, used and politicized. It would even be used as a tool of hate and something to dominate other races and nations and create empires, hence the reference to false prophets. However Christians have to hold on and eventually the Good News about the Kingdom of Heaven (God's self within us) will be spread as a witness to every corner of the world. Then the end will come. The important word here is 'witness' which refers not to the knowledge of, but the demonstration of something.

The reference in the Bible to the **'Beast'**, signified by the code **666**, describes the anti-Christ. It is no doubt a reference to the power of empire, which in the days of Jesus was the Roman Empire ruled by Caesar. But it is a general reference to the prodigal power of Man, the corporate expression of it, best expressed in the rise and fall of consequent grand empires, which seek the salvation of Man through technology, wealth and social control. In the account of the Beast, every person carries the mark of the Beast (666) and no 'trade' can occur without permission of the Beast. Each empire in history becomes more far reaching in its technology (cleverness) and control until the final empire controls the whole world, stifling all freedom and individuality. This 'beast' of corporate power is seen as a potential threat to the spirit of Christ, the concept of the infinite value of the individual and the power of love and forgiveness, freely given, in creating a social cohesion and prosperity. It is a warning that real social cohesion and prosperity comes from our individual capacity to love one another and the Trinity within, rather than corporate dominance of the individuals. The Beast is the concept of the full blown global dictatorship by prodigal Man over the whole world – Satan (the arrogant prodigal Son), in the form of a world corporate body, taking full mastery over his own destiny, controlling every aspect of everyone's life, leaving no room for the life of the Holy Spirit.

Here Jesus has made sure the disciples will not have unsustainable expectations of the message of the Kingdom. They must not lose sight of the purity of his message nor be distracted by other people. He is almost Churchillian in his speech. He is offering only blood, sweat and tears but no surrender, whatever the odds. He is taking a lot of the worry off the shoulders of his followers, by implanting both the true reality of the fight but also that they are on the side of Truth and so will win in the end

– many battles will be lost but the war will be won.

Jesus prepares his followers for a collective horror or trauma of Mankind. He has taught people how to deal with small scale and personal trauma and now he talks of a collective trauma on a large scale. He describes, as the **Awful Horror**, destruction on an epic scale, like the world has never seen and will never see again. People have interpreted this as the destruction of Jerusalem and the scattering of the Jews. However this can be taken to mean that Mankind will suffer catastrophes on a national and eventually global scale that will not destroy Mankind but will make Mankind think it is on the brink of destruction. These events will not be the end of the world because God has 'already reduced the number of days; for if he had not done so, nobody would survive'. The degree to which people perceive such events to be a global threat depends on the masses' understanding of the extent of the world. In Biblical times the destruction of Israel would have seemed like the end of the world, so maybe Jesus started with a reference to the 'Horror standing in the holy place'. To the Jews Israel was the heart of the world. It was a quote from the scriptures; a prophesy people were familiar with. To us living today it would take much more than the destruction of a nation, even our own, to make us panic into thinking the world was ending. So Jesus paints the worst scenario and tells his followers to keep calm and not to panic. There will be a tendency for people to turn in their panic to false Messiahs and charlatans in order to be saved, who will then lead them astray. He is saying, "Hold on!" for the faith he had demonstrated as the Messiah of the Holy Spirit, and which exists in Mankind, is strong enough even for times where all seems lost.

Jesus now takes his disciples through global catastrophes to the end of the earth itself. He says the Son of Man will return, but only at the end of the world, when the physical creation ends. "Where there is a dead body, the vultures shall gather" is a reference to the concept of physical death – his own and the worlds. Such death is not an end, for it is where there is a gathering, a feast or reward. In the chaos of the end the Messiah will come, but it will come as a cosmic revelation or dawning, 'like lightning which flashes across the whole sky from the east to the west'. It is also a reference to Jesus' own resurrection as a man to eternal life, so they know he will be there to again speak for the forgiveness of all Mankind. Here Jesus is averting panic and a terminal loss of faith in the last horrific moments of the earth's existence by saying that they must see it not as a death but a violent birth. He invites his followers again to see these terrible events as positive signs. He eloquently describes these cataclysmic events as being 'the signs of spring in a fig tree as it sprouts green shoots'. You will feel that summer, not horror is just around the corner. He also gives his followers an encouraging image of being saved by being plucked from this nightmare and rescued. "At this time two men will be working in a field; one will be taken away, the other will be left behind". This is obviously not to be taken literally as a physical act but he is saying that those who follow his faith, listen, learn and stay calm will not suffer like those that do not. Be the one who stays calm in the knowledge of their future and you will escape the true terror and suffering of the apocalypse.

Jesus is also perceptive in declaring that the death of the physical world will be sudden and there will be no time to prepare. The extraordinary stability of creation is kept in place by laws. If any laws of the universe are altered, it affects the stability or cohesion of the whole universe. The loss of these physical laws that give us life are such that 'the powers in space will be driven from their courses and stars will fall from heaven'. People will unsuspectingly continue about their business until this sudden collapse occurs. He says that Mankind will be present and will be a witness to the end. He say, "Remember that all these things will happen before the people now living have all died". He is again preparing his followers for anything at any time – not to be surprised. He comforts his followers saying that, "Heaven and earth will pass away (Mankind and all its achievements included) but my words will never pass away". Only then when the physical world disintegrates, will the Son of Man be revealed. Only then will the word be seen clearly; what spiritually is set within us all along, and so physically what we really were. He also says that no one will know, not even him, when the end of time will come. This statement ends all false conjecture and reveals that God the Father will never reveal this through the Holy Spirit to even the prodigal Son. It is taken on trust that such knowledge is not helpful to the prodigally aware Son.

The Judgement

Jesus swept away the notion of the Kingdom of Heaven as something external to ourselves. He defined heaven as the experience of self, God's self or the Trinity within us. Heaven was the humble prodigal Son in unity or redeemed with the Father in the shared person of the Holy Spirit. He said that a person cannot enter the Kingdom of Heaven, 'unless he be born again in the spirit'. Hell was the arrogant prodigal Son without the redeeming help of the Father in the person of the Holy Spirit.

In Jesus' stories people store up riches in heaven here and now; people accept invites to wedding feasts here and now; people go to work in the vineyard here and now; people are born again in the spirit here and now. The thief that was crucified beside Jesus felt he had nowhere to go. His humility won him a trip with Jesus to paradise – 'today'.

Jesus, although he talked of eternal damnation and hell, actually removed the concept of hell. He saw the life of the prodigal Sons or forms of Satan and all his demons as self inflicted illusions. The prodigal state was in fact a state of 'not being alive'. So Jesus calls people to wake up, be born, come alive. He saw us as souls, vessels to be filled or 'names'. Our names were either given Life and were filled with God's self or not. They were either 'written in heaven' or not. We either came to the wedding feast or stayed away. He saw hell not as a place of cruel, pointless and eternal suffering but an invite not taken up; a place setting not occupied; an invite blowing discarded in the gutter with our name written on it. The concept of **not** taking up a soul or not taking a seat at a feast is a difficult concept for the living to understand – being already dead or absent. It is easier to conceive of annihilation or punishment but not easy to conceive of never being 'born' at all; of being invited to live but passing it by. So the concept of hell is an anathema – people's souls, invites, places are simply given to others. Resurrection cannot be given to those who never lived. Of course people can be forgiven for not taking up their invite and experience eternal life but they cannot be given an eternal life of condemnation.

Jesus, ever the good teacher, uses the familiar approach he knows will work, as he wanders around with his invites; cajoling and pushing people toward the party, he uses the carrot and stick. He assures people of the reality of the party and its Life, makes people feel worthy and welcome but also tells them it is the only party in town. He cannot warn people or describe hell as a place of 'not being born', of **nothingness**. It is incomprehensible. So he has to produce a concept of hell that is comprehensible – comprising of **something**. A stick that is nothing cannot be used! So he says if they pass Life by, there is nothing else on. He describes hell as a place of exclusion, of darkness, the closest imagery to nothingness. He says people will be sorry for refusing Life, even though they will never know it – 'there will be wailing and gnashing of teeth'. The Life they think they have is a trick and if they ever knew what they were missing they would feel indescribable disappointment.

Jesus talks of his Father's house as having many rooms. This is a reference to heaven not being a homogenous place. It is limitlessly accommodating. It is a reference to its perfection not being something exclusive and selective, but a perfection that is infinitely inclusive and varied – a forgiving and generous rather than a miserly perfection ... a perfect harmony of diverse parts.

Jesus talks of varying wealth in heaven, although everyone receives the same prize – eternal life. The humblest will be made great and the great will be made small. He says even if someone gives one of his followers a cup of water, he will be rewarded with much more in heaven. He says to his disciples that if they give up farms, families and the riches of this life, they will be repaid with much more in heaven. They will be given cities in return. He is saying that even if people are hugely rich in this life, it is nothing compared to the wealth in heaven. The wealth inherited in the Kingdom is the respect, importance and significance that your name affords – and the power that goes with it.

Jesus says that 'sinners and prostitutes will be finding their way into the Kingdom of Heaven before righteous people'. This is because heaven is only for the humble. It is for those that know that they do not and cannot, on their own, deserve heaven. He tells people to sit at the back of the hall on Judgement Day and be humble. Jesus seeks out the arrogance in people. Heaven is not a reward for the deserving, righteous and hard working; heaven cannot be earned. All righteousness, hard work and service are unpaid as these are what we owe anyway. Jesus tells a story of some faithful Christians who seek him out at the end of time crying, "Lord, Lord" and relating to him all their achievements, including miracles, they had performed in his name. Jesus tells them to go away saying, "I do not know you. Go away you wicked people". Jesus' dismissal is absolute and without explanation or discussion. This is because they have misunderstood the Kingdom of God's Self. It is granted freely as something already within us. It is not a reward. What the Prodigal Son gives to the Kingdom should be also similarly freely given. They were arrogant and did not see that what they had done was something they owed God anyway. They did not show humility for all that they did not do.

Hell is described by Jesus as a place not for the un-forgiven but the unforgiving. It is for the arrogant, the people who think they deserve heaven. Jesus tells people to rank themselves below the worst sinner. This is not a false modesty but a realisation that true humility is the acceptance of each person's equal culpability in Original, and therefore all sin. The people who think they are chosen are not humble and do so to escape the responsibility of humility. Jesus tells people that to call another man a fool, let alone evil, puts them in danger of hellfire. One prodigal Son cannot criticise another for their prodigal nature. Everyone, including Jesus himself, is born into Original Sin (awareness) and so temptation and so everyone equally depends on grace and redemption.

The dead are not aware they are dead until they see Life. Jesus has to treat people, who he is persuading to take Life (or be born), as if they were alive, capable of seeing Life. So he describes Hell (as people have to) as a 'place' to avoid. So Jesus describes it as a place, which it is not. It is a state of being 'unborn'.

There is a problem with the juxtaposition of Love and the punishment of a conscious eternal damnation. Establishment churches had a huge social, political and economic power and they no doubt used this threat of eternal damnation (unimaginable suffering) in order to subdue and frighten the ignorant masses into submission and swell their congregation – and so the coffers. The measures the churches took to save souls from this terrible damnation suggested that they believed little in damnation themselves. However there was also no doubt a genuine desire to expand the knowledge of the Trinity and the church knew it had to use whatever 'tools in the bag' that worked. Jesus himself encouraged his future church to do just this by saying, "Take out old and new truths" – i.e. do whatever it takes. This also meant having the courage to change one's tune when no-one is listening. When he gave Peter the job of 'feeding his sheep', he gave him full doctrinal freedom so his church might dress up the message of humility in whatever form they felt might be most palatable. The Truth is of no use if it is not palatable.

Jesus tells a story about the nature of Man's failure to grasp the 'here and now', to see the Kingdom of Heaven as 'here and now' – and its consequences. He tells a story of a **rich man who**

was unforgiving to the poor. He dies and realises he is suffering now himself by being a victim of his own lack of forgiveness. He wants to come back to earth and warn his brother. He is told he cannot go because there is nothing he can offer his brother. His brother already has the advice of the prophets and he is not listening. Why should he listen to his dead brother? Jesus is not saying here that people do actually go to a place of suffering. He is telling a story to explain why God, even if people did live in afterlife of hell, would not allow them to come back and warn their friends. People in fact find it grossly unfair (even illogical) that there is no afterlife from which people can return and warn their friends of the Truth and so find Salvation. If it were allowed, then the rich man might give to the poor (and tick all the right boxes) just to get into the Kingdom of Heaven. But this is exactly why there is no afterlife – only a resurrection of our 'names' or souls at the end of time. Salvation, finding the Trinity within or being 'born again in the spirit' comes by our own humility alone. God does not want people to listen to the deaf and blind from beyond the grave and make deceitful responses out of fear of punishment or reward that is to come. He wants us to see and listen to what the prophets see and hear. He wants the people to tick boxes only because they want to in a response to a sense of their own humility, and the love and duty that springs from it. Prophets tell of the Holy Spirit of the Trinity within people which saves people from themselves, not some carefully orchestrated religion – or a warning from the grave. The Holy Spirit (the person of will) cannot frighten either the prodigal Son or the Father into cooperation, but serves only their **common** desire. It can only give what it receives. Jesus makes the point that the Trinity lies within people now and in all the creation around them. If they do not see it here and now, what makes them think they will recognise it in some afterlife, even if there was one?

Jesus is telling us here why **re-incarnation** is not a part of God's creation and the Trinity. This is because the idea that people save themselves by the personal accumulation and attainment of some knowledge, righteousness or Godhead is wrong. People are saved by 'being born again in the Holy Spirit', by being completely humble in their own will. This is the realisation that they cannot be righteous by their own will, however many lives they have. They need the will of the loving Father and the humility of their own will realised in the Person of will – the Holy Spirit. This is the only warning that the brother could give if he returned from the dead, and this is being said by the prophets. The brother has to claim the Holy Spirit and its help, by his own humility, by his own will – here and now.

At Judgement Day the **last shall be first and the first shall be last.** This is a reference to the separation or chasm that is created between the spiritual and physical by the prodigal Son. Only the Holy Spirit can bridge this chasm and unite them. In the Holy Spirit, the seeming weakness and meekness of the spiritual (the believer) will be found to have power – the last shall be first. The great power of the physical (the unbeliever) will be found to be worthless – the first shall be last. Jesus joins the two together in his statement – "Render to Caesar that which is Caesar's and to God that which is God's". Invest in both but remember the respective value of each. Do not offer humility to Caesar for he does not want it and do not offer what Caesar has to God for He does not want it. But serve both with what they want.

Jesus says that **many will be called but few will be chosen.** He says that the road to perdition is wide but few will choose the narrow gate to Life. Jesus paints a gloomy picture of the salvation of Mankind. This however is the realistic and truthful picture. We almost all fail miserably the challenge of the Trinity within us – its reality for us. At the end of the day we will all need to 'throw ourselves at the mercy of the court'. We will all be disappointed in ourselves, when we see the reality before us. Jesus attacked the three demons that cut us off from the forgiveness that will save us and others – complacency, arrogance and hypocrisy. They blind us to our humility and so our salvation – the love and forgiveness of the Father shared in the Holy Spirit.

The **parable of the wedding feast** warns us of these demons. In this story Jesus attacks the Jewish notion (or any religious notion) that people are 'chosen'. He loathed it for its complacency and arrogance. In the story a King (God) announces a wedding feast and sends out invites. Those that have invites (the chosen Jews) are too complacent and busy to come for they consider the prize is already theirs. So the King sends out his servants (the Holy Spirit) to invite and drag in anybody they find off the street (the un-chosen or Gentiles). God invites the world to his feast – everyone has the Trinity within. Only those in wedding clothes are chosen or let in to the wedding in the end. These clothes are symbolic of the marriage or unity of the Father, Son and Holy Spirit. The feast is symbolic of the Kingdom of Heaven or unity of this Trinity of persons. The people who are let in are those humble enough to realise that they do not deserve to be present and are invited only by the love and generosity of the King. We can feel the rage of Jesus when he describes the arrogant being barred from the feast. They gnash their teeth and tear their fine clothes in grief in the cold and dark outside.

Judgement therefore is at the end of time. This is because people cannot be judged in isolation but all together. We are judged in the context of the whole story. Jesus says in the **parable of the weeds** that people cannot be separated before the end of time (the harvest time) because the good maybe thrown out with the bad. If we try to pull up weeds which are amongst corn, we may pull up the corn too. Good and bad is entwined together and can only be separated at the end when all lives have been lived. There is reason, logic or Truth to the Final Judgement.

There are good and bad spirits or notions in people's souls which result in good and bad responses. People would be diminished or disrupted by the removal of the bad spirits (products of prodigal self) but the good survives whilst the bad is exposed as illusionary and worthless at the end. So a judgement or separation of good and bad cannot occur in the life of the world just as it cannot occur within our lifetime. Our actions grow beyond our own lives through time and beyond our death. Jesus talks of spirits or notions as yeast that multiplies. We might see them as ripples in a pond. Jesus says small sins need to be nipped in the bud because they can grow into something that far outweighs and obscures the good in our soul. He tells people 'if your eye offends you, pluck it out. It is better to enter the Kingdom of Heaven eyeless than not at all'. So Jesus reminds us of the power of small and seemingly insignificant acts of sin or goodness to go a very long way. For example the effect of Jesus exposing the Holy Spirit in his life has grown to huge proportions in the lives of subsequent generations. Even Jesus asks people, and wonders himself, how much of the faith he has sown will be found at the end of time. "Will I find faith on earth at the end of time?" We could ask the same of our own actions. In a film on the Nuremberg trials, Spencer Tracey plays a defending lawyer for a German judge who is on trial. He interviewed the judge, who was accused of condemning people to death illegally. The judge said he was truly sorry for what had happened and never realised that it would all lead to such horror. Spencer Tracey replied, "It all came to this the day you sent the first innocent man to his death". When we harm a person we harm much more than that person and when we forgive someone we forgive much more than that one person. We change the story.

God has different expectations of each person. Jesus was given a role in the story that he took on. He could have rejected it. If someone has a spirit or 'talent' it is what they do with it in the story that matters. In the **parable of the talents** the three servants have differing amounts to invest. It is their own varying willingness to invest what they have that is the important, not what they have. So the effect of their investment is what is under judgement not what they have. Again it is what goes beyond their lives that is judged. If someone just serves themselves with what they have to themselves, then it is taken from them and given to someone who will invest it. God is economic with His resources and nothing is wasted. This principle is repeated in the **story of the orchard owner,** who wants to cut down and burn a tree that produces no fruit. A worker pleads for the tree to be given a second chance. The owner tells him to manure the tree and if no fruit is produced the next year, then he must cut it down and replace it. Jesus is saying that 'those to whom much is given, much is expected'. Jesus is alluding to the Trinity as not something we have for ourselves but all share in – a fellowship of all people. We have to see ourselves not just in terms of our own lives but in terms of all lives, past, present and future. If a person is not prepared to serve the fellowship, it will find someone who will. This is echoed by the words, "Thy will be done" in the Lord's Prayer.

Jesus says that people only come to him, "if they are drawn by the Father". This again suggests the predominance of spirits in our lives. We are called to fulfil or deliver a story. Jesus says he was sent here. He talked after his baptism of being 'born again in the spirit' (receiving the Holy Spirit) as if he were only a spirit. He talks in such terms as, "I will go.... be taken up.... raised up". Judas fulfilled the story (the scriptures) in a way that could be seen as evil, but Jesus says it took place so 'that the scriptures should be fulfilled and the Son of Man glorified'. It was so God may be demonstrated to Mankind. So it proves only God knows what each person is given and what is expected and what may or may not be their judgement.

The resurrected Jesus is deemed as being a part of that Final Judgement. The reason for this is that Jesus was prodigal Man reunited with the Father, in the Holy Spirit by virtue of his own humility. He therefore earned the right to sit as the Son on the right hand of the Father by virtue of his own humility. He is equipped to judge the humility of the prodigal Son's return to the Kingdom. On the cross he took on his full responsibility as a prodigal Son (so full humility) for Original Sin or Mankind's (everyone's) prodigal sin, so he has the right to forgive anybody and everyone, as the Father. This right extends to everyone – both B.C. and A.D.

Chapter Ten

Hypocrisy

Walking the walk

Arrogance and complacency were stumbling blocks to humility. Hypocrisy however was the real threat to his Truth – its deception and dishonesty. Jesus was intolerant of people who dressed up a lie as the Truth and so deceived both themselves and others. Dishonesty or self deception was at the heart of the Fall of Man – the lie that the prodigal Son can exist without the persons of the loving Father and Holy Spirit or Helper. Jesus did not have any anger against Caesar or the government of the day. He forgave injustice but not the dressing up of injustice as justice. Jesus asked his followers to completely integrate with Caesar, the prodigal world and the law of the land. However he asked his followers to give to God that which is God's – their humility, which ultimately means being wholly honest, particularly with oneself.

Jesus hated the Pharisees, the religious masters of the day who displayed an outside perfection and self approval and asked that people follow strictly their religious standard, but failed those standards themselves. The Pharisees, Sadducees, Levites and lawyers were the people who had power in society and were guardians of the faith, justice and truth. They were entrusted to look after these important matters for the poor and vulnerable and they abused it openly. Instead of giving people faith and justice, they accumulated power, wealth and privilege. This hypocrisy was at the heart of Jesus' violence and anger directed at the money lenders and hawkers who ripped off the poor pilgrims in the Temple. Jesus physically threw them out.

Jesus separates his Truth (and so his followers) from that of the Pharisees. He speaks of a new code of behaviour to root out this hypocrisy. Jesus asks them (describing the Pharisees), "What use is it to clean the outside of the cup if the inside is not clean?" He tells his followers that 'everything that is done in the dark will be brought into the light and exposed'. He tells them that it is as bad to lust after a girl as to commit adultery; as bad to be angry with someone as to actually harm them physically. Jesus is not setting cruel and impossible standards but pointing out the importance of humility and the honesty it demands. Honesty is the reasoning behind the **story of the widow's mite**. The rich man gives a huge bag of money to charity and leaves smugly, bathing in the glow of Caesar's adoration (his own generosity) – but it is only ten percent of his wealth. The widow gives a tiny penny but it is all she has. The widow is honestly generous and the rich man is dishonestly generous. Also the widow is the one who has done the will of God – shown absolute generosity. The rich man has pretended to do so. Jesus is angered by the rich man's dishonesty.

Honesty is the reasoning behind Jesus' call to a fellowship that seems impossible: "Love your enemy; do good to those that harm you; lend without any thought of return; give to anyone all that they ask; if someone strikes you, turn the other cheek; if someone steals your shirt, give them your coat also....." . Such a model would bring down 'Caesar' – nations, churches, families, banking systems. So we see Jesus separate church from state and command people to serve 'Caesar's' demands. Jesus is pointing out the innocent and infinite generosity of God's love, the Father's love; how he treats the prodigal Son. The prodigal or aware Son can **only** offer his humility in the glare of such 'impossible' generosity; his absolute honesty about his own failure before the Father. Only in this state of humility and honesty can he be helped, can he find grace to achieve this impossible righteousness, to partake in miracles.

Jesus tells a story about two men who each built a house, one on sand and one on rock. The one who built on sand lost his house when a storm blew and washed the house away. The one built on rock survived. This was the house built on the rock of humility and honesty. This is the rock that has the help of the Holy Spirit. This humility means the prodigal Son cannot judge or condemn another, simply because we all fail the test of absolute generosity, however righteous we may be. When Jesus saves the adulterous woman from being stoned to death he demonstrates this. He says to the men who prepare to stone her, "Let the man without sin cast the first stone". Each man slowly retreats (the eldest first!), until they are alone. He asks the woman, "Who condemns you now?" She replies, "None". Jesus counts himself amongst the prodigal (albeit saved by his own humility) when he says, "then neither do I". When a rich and self righteous man calls Jesus 'good', he rebukes him. "Do not call me good, for only God is good". Jesus is being honest about himself as a prodigal Son; that he is not righteously perfect but humble. By his humility, not his 'goodness' does he receive help from the Father by the Holy Spirit.

Jesus taunts the Pharisees and their obsession with their own righteousness. He tells them they are like people who 'strain their food to keep out a gnat and end up by swallowing a camel". Again this is a mocking reference to their reliance on religion to keep themselves clean rather than their own humility and the help of the Holy Spirit. Such people pore over the scriptures to find out what they should do or not do and then fail to keep out the biggest sin of all – our arrogant prodigal nature and its lack of absolute generosity. Jesus undermines the Pharisees tendency to preach and tell other people how to live their lives. They notice a small sin or 'splinter' in someone's eye and then are unable to help them because of the plank in their own eye. Again this plank is a reference to a lack of humility and generosity – the honesty of our own prodigal failure. Only their sharing in humility and the Holy Spirit can hope to get the splinter out of the man's eye. Only the knowledge of humility and the Helper that comes to its aid can save the prodigal Son. He tells the Pharisees that 'they cross the seas to convert people and make them twice as fit for hell as they were'. He is not saying that these converts will go to hell for believing the Pharisees, but that they are made 'fit' for hell. He is blaming the Pharisees not just for hindering people but for doing great harm. He is accusing them of putting planks into people's eyes.

Jesus angers the Pharisees and religious authorities when he ignores the Sabbath. He is seen to be healing the sick and plucking a few ears of corn to eat. No work of any kind was permitted on the Sabbath. Jesus tells the people that, "the Sabbath was made for Man, not Man for the Sabbath". He is saying here that all laws should be implemented and observed for the sole purpose of helping Man, not for the sake of making Man's life difficult. They should be there for the purpose of helping Man get the most out of life. Jesus is introducing the concept of 'the spirit of the law', which was a completely new concept – that laws are made for Man rather than Man being made for laws. This was considered subversive to the rule of law.

Jesus warned the disciples against the 'yeast of the Pharisees', as he called it. He said to the man who was born blind and he had healed, "I came to this world to judge, so that the blind should see and those that see should be made blind". He had come to judge or show what the real truth about faith was and expose the lies of the Pharisees. He would reveal that the lies of the Pharisees made people blind and he would make them see. He would show that the Pharisees, who everyone believes can see, are in fact blind. God was a Spirit living within all people and for whom all people could testify.

It is reported in Matthew that Jesus rails against the Pharisees, "How terrible for you, the teachers of the law and the Pharisees! You hypocrites! You lock the door to the Kingdom of Heaven in people's faces and you yourselves do not go in, nor do you allow in those that are trying to enter". He also accuses the teachers of the Law of 'keeping the key (narrow gate) to the

Kingdom of Heaven from people'. Here Jesus sums up his bitterness and frustration. These people actively hinder people's entry to the Kingdom of Heaven by their hypocrisy. He describes some of their practices that have no religious sense. He asks why, if someone swears by the Temple, then the vow is not binding but if he swears by the gold in the Temple, then it is binding. What, he asks, makes the gold holy? Surely it is the Temple! Similarly he asks why, if someone swears by the altar, then it is not binding but if he swears by the gift on the altar (which is brought), it is binding. Is it not the altar that makes the gift holy? He is attacking the greed of the Pharisees. He rages that the Pharisees may give a ten percent tithe to the Temple but do not uphold justice, mercy and honesty. He says that they 'strain out a fly only to swallow a camel'. Jesus sees tithing as a good thing but nowhere as important as justice and mercy. He says that this value system is as useless as washing a cup on the outside and not on the inside.

Jesus then goes to town and attacks the practices of the Church full on. He says that they are the authorised interpreters of Moses' law. He tells people to do what they are told to do by the Pharisees but not to imitate their lifestyle. This is a clever distinction. He knows that they do not practice what they preach! They burden people with their demands and laws but do nothing to help them carry these burdens. They are show offs. They wear long tassels on their cloaks and large straps (with scriptures written on them) on their foreheads and arms. Both these are marks of great devotion to scripture and God which they show proudly off to everyone. They take the best seats at weddings and in the synagogue. They like to be called Teacher and be greeted with respect in public.

Jesus counters this arrogance, complacency and hypocrisy with a startling act of humility. He washes the feet of his disciples. This is an act normally carried out by a woman of the lowest of servants. The disciples are shocked but Jesus tells them that if they want to be leaders they must serve humbly. In heaven the humble shall be made great and the great will be humbled. Each man must serve the other with what they have been given with the humility of a servant. He tells them that people in his fellowship must not be called teacher or Father as they will have a Father and a teacher (the Holy Spirit) within them. All people will be members of one family. No-one will be called leader but himself which is fitting as there can be only one leader in a revolution – the first man to go forward. All people, even though others may do greater works than himself by the Holy Spirit, follow his first example.

Chapter Eleven

Jesus Today

It is said that there is not one contemporary account of Jesus. Everything was written after his death – generally decades or centuries after. This is strange and it opens up an opportunity for a mystery – a questioning of whether he was a real man or myth. It invites us to make an even handed choice – either to believe in the man or the myth.

This historical choice exactly mirrors the choice that the Truth of the Trinity, the concept of who we are, presents to us. It is the same as pondering whether the wine in Cana was real or not. It actually does not matter whether it is real or not. Caesar's science (the prodigal world) would say it does matter and, with regard to what Caesar wishes to achieve and do, it does matter. But Jesus was not trying to save a wedding feast. Jesus wanted to demonstrate something about our sense of self – its ability to generate its own reality. Just as it can trick itself into believing in something that is not there (the wine), it can trick itself into **not** seeing something that is there (the Trinity) – simply by its own will.

It is our will that, at the end of the day, can decide what reality is and what it is not. It is we who can see the Holy Spirit's help, or not. Jesus says that oaths should not be made on people or books but we should say simply either yes or no. He is saying that it is our will alone that has the power to say yes or no, to see or not see, to make a choice. No worship, deification, love, knowledge or dedication of a person (even Jesus), a book (the Torah, Bible or Koran) or a fellowship (any church) will draw us closer to, or convince us of, the existence of our humility and so the Helper – only our own honest choice to be or not be. This freedom is at the heart of the love of God and the help of the Holy Spirit. It is the spirit of the Helper. St. Paul said that people could blaspheme against the Father and the Son but to blaspheme against the Holy Spirit was unforgivable. The freedom to say 'yes or no' is the sacred heart of the Christian faith, the Father's Love, the inheritance of the Son, the help of the Holy Spirit. Love not freely given and received is not Love. If someone threatens this Spirit of freedom of the Christian world, there would be war, whatever the cost.

There is a place in Peter Pan where Barrie the author tells us that the lost children felt that they belonged to no-one. So they sat around and said 'jaggy things'. It is an astute observation on the nature of Mankind. A sense of being on our own isolates the sense of self and brings a defensiveness and fear. We are put on our guard, feeling we have to take care of ourselves. We become 'jaggy'. People crave to belong – to escape the jaggy or prodigal world of 'dog eat dog'. Deep down they seek salvation or a sense of belonging. However perfect in its attempts, Caesar or the secular (humanism) cannot make us feel less abandoned or 'jaggy'. It cannot fill this void, the knowledge of inevitable futility and failure. However proficient, the secular cannot create a true unity or fellowship for it cannot transcend the futility of the physical. It can only impart physical short term solutions. However perfect those physical solutions seem, they do not cure us of our 'depression' or of being lost, jaggy, abandoned children.

H. G. Wells, the author, famously called religion 'pickled God'. Like many of us he did not subscribe to the notion of a supernatural God somewhere out there or a supernatural God somewhere down here in the form of the man Jesus. However he did say that although he was an atheist by religious standards he did feel that 'the whole history of Mankind revolves around this one man (Jesus)'. Wells touched on the essence or simple

Truth, encapsulated by Jesus the man, as being something at the very heart of Mankind's story – around which all revolves. He did not see Jesus as a genetically supernatural man physically come down to earth to demonstrate a supernatural God through a supernatural life, to which the rest of Mankind can only be a mere useless spectator. He sensed that Jesus was a man physically the same as all of us, born into a prodigal world, but who by the simple choice of humility redeemed himself of his prodigal nature and so revealed the Trinity of self within all Mankind – with all its limitless possibilities.

It was in this Truth that Jesus put his absolute faith, which enabled him to give his followers complete freedom and control over the shape of it on earth. In every age Jesus is unconcerned by the shape of religious doctrine. Questions as to whether for example it is right for women to preach or not, the rights and wrongs of marriage, homosexuality etc are entirely answered by the question, "Does the shape of the doctrine (truths) help or hinder the message?". In one age or culture a doctrine (truth) will help and in another hinder or distort the message. So Jesus told his followers to not be afraid to bring new **and** old 'truths' from out of the storeroom. Because we change a truth or doctrine it does not mean that the old truth was wrong and the new truth is right. Jesus says that old truths (doctrines) may indeed be reintroduced if needs be. A truth or doctrine, whether new or old, is simply a tool that helps make the 'face' of the message or Word, recognisable and digestible to people.

The message, Truth or Word itself never changes – that love or unity without free will is not love, nor unity. The full extent of all creation or existence, whatever it might be revealed to be, is completely meaningless and void without a sense of its own self. That sense of self can only come into existence through the unity of the three persons (biblically described as the Father, Son and Holy Spirit or the Kingdom of Heaven) by free will or love. The power and presence of God therefore lies in this sense of self alone and this lies within everything. God therefore only exists as a Trinity, sense of self or spirit of Love – in every part of all creation. Jesus describes this Trinity of self present within people as a divinity, which is boundless and has immeasurable value, with his words, "What does it profit a man if he gains the world but loses his soul?". He is saying that it is the Trinity of self (a soul) within us that gives us the world (Life), not the other way around. He leaves us in no doubt of this eternal, boundless soul or Life in the 'proof' or **Truth** that lies within the **parable of the Sower**.

It is therefore of this parable that Jesus says, "If you cannot comprehend this parable then how can you comprehend the others?" Jesus is saying that the parable describes the 'Truth' or comprehension of the Trinity or Kingdom of Heaven, and all his teachings are based on this parable.

In this parable Jesus reveals the identity of the Prodigal Son. In owning up to the Prodigal Son within (whether the Brute, Snake or Lucifer) as an expression of self consciousness (Original Sin) we can then see the Trinity of Self, Kingdom of Heaven, the Father, Son and Holy Spirit or God's self within. In owning up to the Prodigal Son within we are 'born again'. We see God's Self as holographical and so universal, as much within us as without us. We see the Prodigal Son redeemed by entering into a full partnership with the Father and both their wills in the partnership of the Holy Spirit – a common person with a common will.

This process of owning up to or recognising the Prodigal Son or Person is immortalised by Jesus' call to "Pick up thy cross (the Prodigal Self) and follow me". In the parable of the Sower the Prodigal Sons who do not bear fruit, recognise the Father that is outside them and so not the Prodigal Self of themselves. They do not see the Father, Prodigal Son and Holy Spirit as a partnership of persons or selves within them. The Kingdom of Heaven is hidden from them. The person of the 'good soil' admits to the Prodigal self and so does not try to avoid it, change it or eradicate it but allows it, by virtue of his own will (share in the Holy Spirit) to be embraced in a partnership with the Father and Holy Spirit. He accepts his true self as God's self.

Jesus identifies in this parable the indivisibility and so unity of flesh (the physical) and spirit. They are one world, as they always have been, are now, and always will be. The Kingdom of Heaven is a limitless but unified expression of one universal Self – God's Self. It constantly evolves and changes, creating and recreating, as one unified Self. As one part of creation is born or dies God's self is not born nor dies for all things are God's self and God conscious. Such events are changes in the expression of God's Self - the changing face of God if you like. Only in the self consciousness of the Prodigal Son are spirit and flesh sensed as separate to each other.

Only in the Prodigal Son does the Father, Son and the person of their wills (the Holy Spirit) or God's Self become divided. Only in the prodigal self consciousness of man does God's consciousness become eclipsed along with the knowledge of its own universality. Only the Prodigal Son therefore experiences death or extinction.

In redemption or rebirth however this Prodigal Son can experience the eternal life of God's Self. In resurrection an individual is granted their self consciousness or 'name' but not only of the Prodigal Self but of God's Self or the Kingdom of Heaven. In the Kingdom of Heaven individuals share the same self as all creation but retain their self consciousness - their 'names' only. In the future we retain within our 'names' what we have already within us now - the Father, Son and Holy Spirit or God's self. The Kingdom of Heaven is the paradoxical experience of an individual self and its self consciousness or 'name' and its oneness with, unity or complete belonging to one eternal shared Self – God's Self. In Jesus' words 'our names are written in Heaven' – our self consciousness is accepted as a part of the eternal face of God.

Entry into the Kingdom of Heaven or God's self is therefore a simple act of witness or acknowledgement of the holographic and so universal presence of God's self, as a Trinity, in all things – an act of belief in the universal presence of the Spirit of Love or Holy Spirit.

Printed in the United Kingdom
by Lightning Source UK Ltd.
126643UK00001BA/51/P